GRAPHIC HISTORY

JOHN SUTTER
★ AND THE ★
CALIFORNIA
GOLD RUSH

by Matt Doeden
illustrated by Ron Frenz
and Charles Barnett III

Consultant:
John Mark Lambertson
Director and Archivist
National Frontier Trails Museum
Independence, Missouri

Capstone
press
Mankato, Minnesota

Graphic Library is published by Capstone Press,
1710 Roe Crest Drive, North Mankato, Minnesota 56003.
www.capstonepub.com

Library of Congress Cataloging-in-Publication Data
Doeden, Matt.
John Sutter and the California gold rush / by Matt Doeden; illustrated by Ron Frenz and Charles Barnett, III.
p. cm.—(Graphic library. Graphic history)
Summary: In graphic novel format, tells the story of the discovery of gold at John Sutter's mill and how it changed California.
Includes bibliographical references and index.
ISBN: 978-0-7368-4370-6 (hardcover)
ISBN: 978-0-7368-6207-3 (softcover pbk.)
1. California—Gold discoveries—Juvenile literature. 2. Sutter, John Augustus, 1803–1880—Juvenile literature. I. Barnett, Charles, III ill. II. Frenz, Ron ill. III. Title. IV. Series.
F865.D63 2006
979.4'04—dc22 2005007890

Art and Editorial Direction
Jason Knudson and Blake A. Hoena

Designers
Bob Lentz and Kate Opseth

Colorist
Ben Hunzeker

Editor
Christopher Harbo

Editor's note: Direct quotations from primary sources are indicated by a yellow background.

Direct quotations appear on the following pages:
Page 6, from *Gold Dust and Gunsmoke: Tales of Gold Rush Outlaws, Gunfighters, Lawmen, and Vigilantes* by John Boessenecker (New York: John Wiley, 1999).
Page 27, from "The Discovery of Gold in California" by General John Sutter, *Hutchings' California Magazine*, 1857 (http://www.sfmuseum.org/hist2/gold.html).

Printed in the United States 4634

TABLE OF CONTENTS

Chapter 1
Sutter's Mill

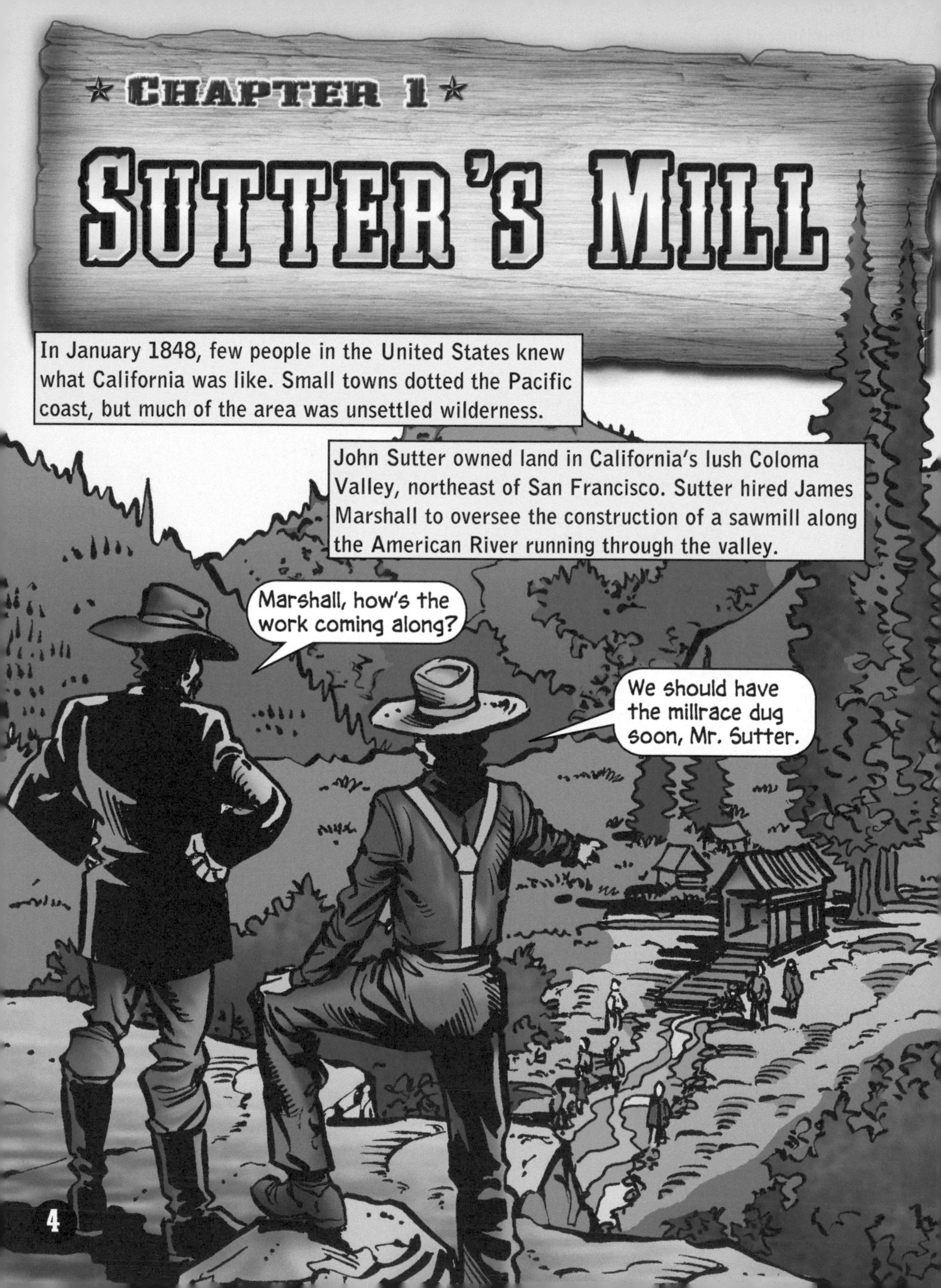
In January 1848, few people in the United States knew what California was like. Small towns dotted the Pacific coast, but much of the area was unsettled wilderness.
John Sutter owned land in California's lush Coloma Valley, northeast of San Francisco. Sutter hired James Marshall to oversee the construction of a sawmill along the American River running through the valley.
Marshall, how's the work coming along?
We should have the millrace dug soon, Mr. Sutter.

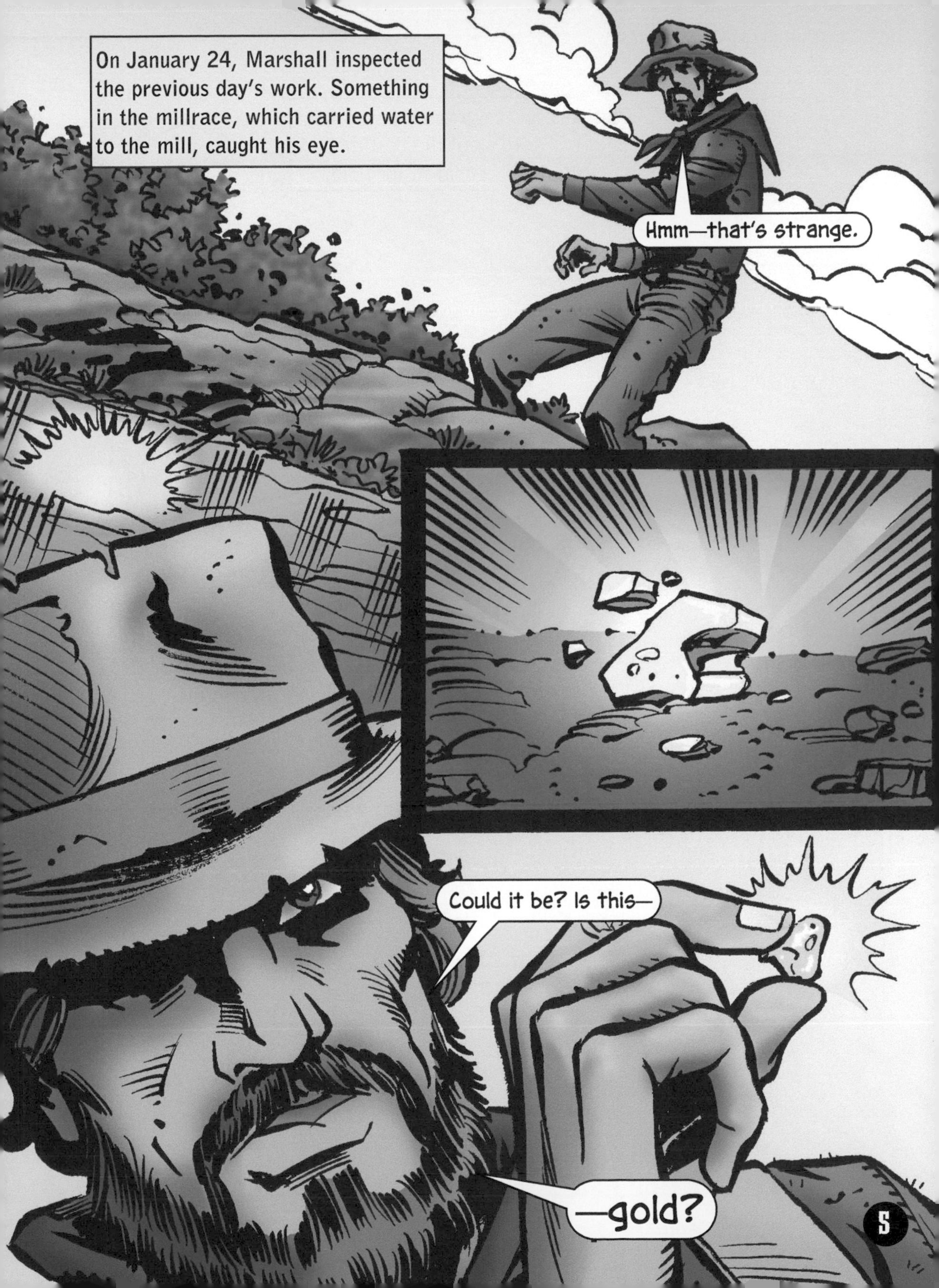
On January 24, Marshall inspected the previous day's work. Something in the millrace, which carried water to the mill, caught his eye.
Hmm—that's strange.
Could it be? Is this—
—gold?

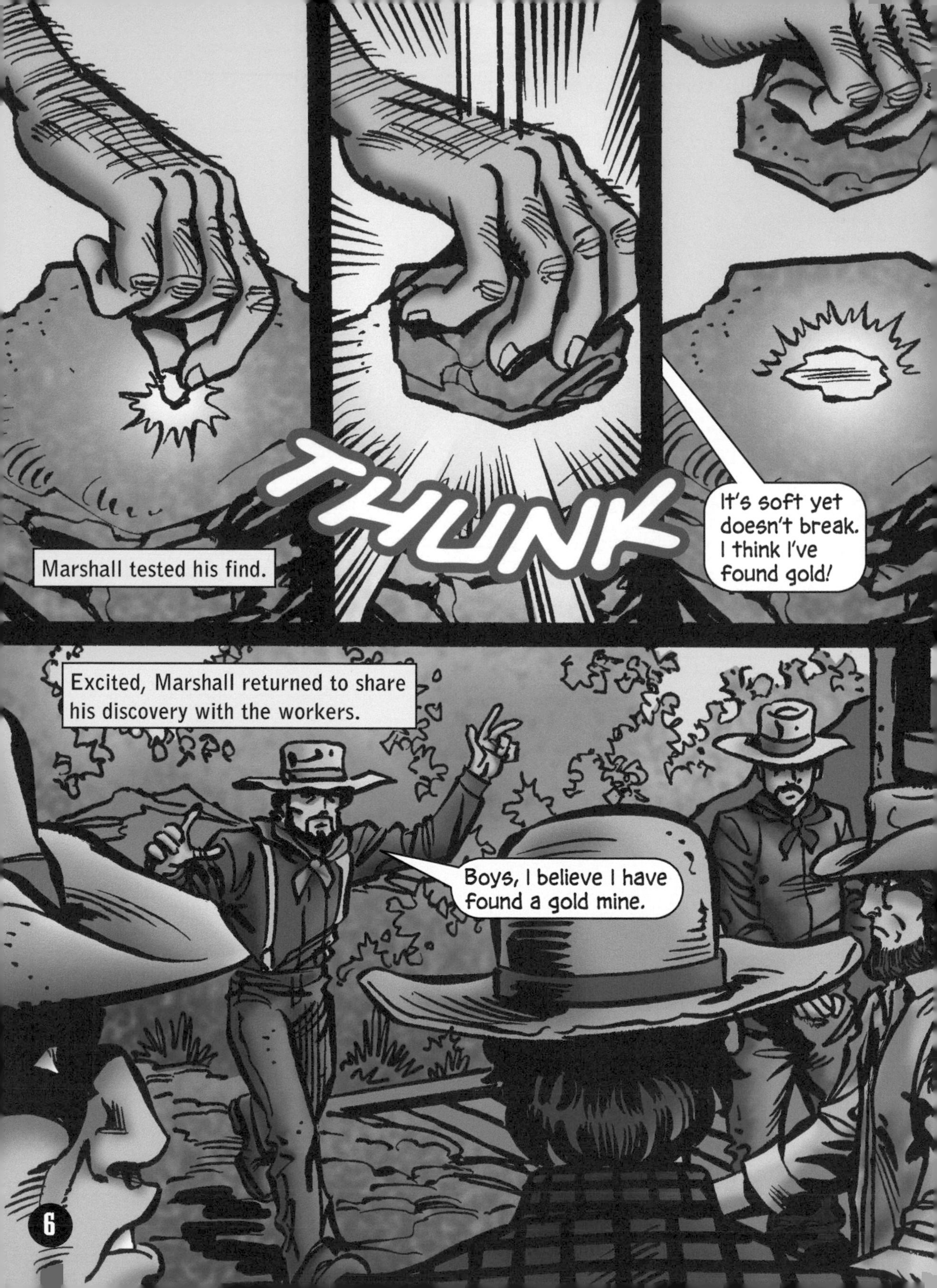
Marshall tested his find.
THUNK
It's soft yet doesn't break. I think I've found gold!
Excited, Marshall returned to share his discovery with the workers.
Boys, I believe I have found a gold mine.

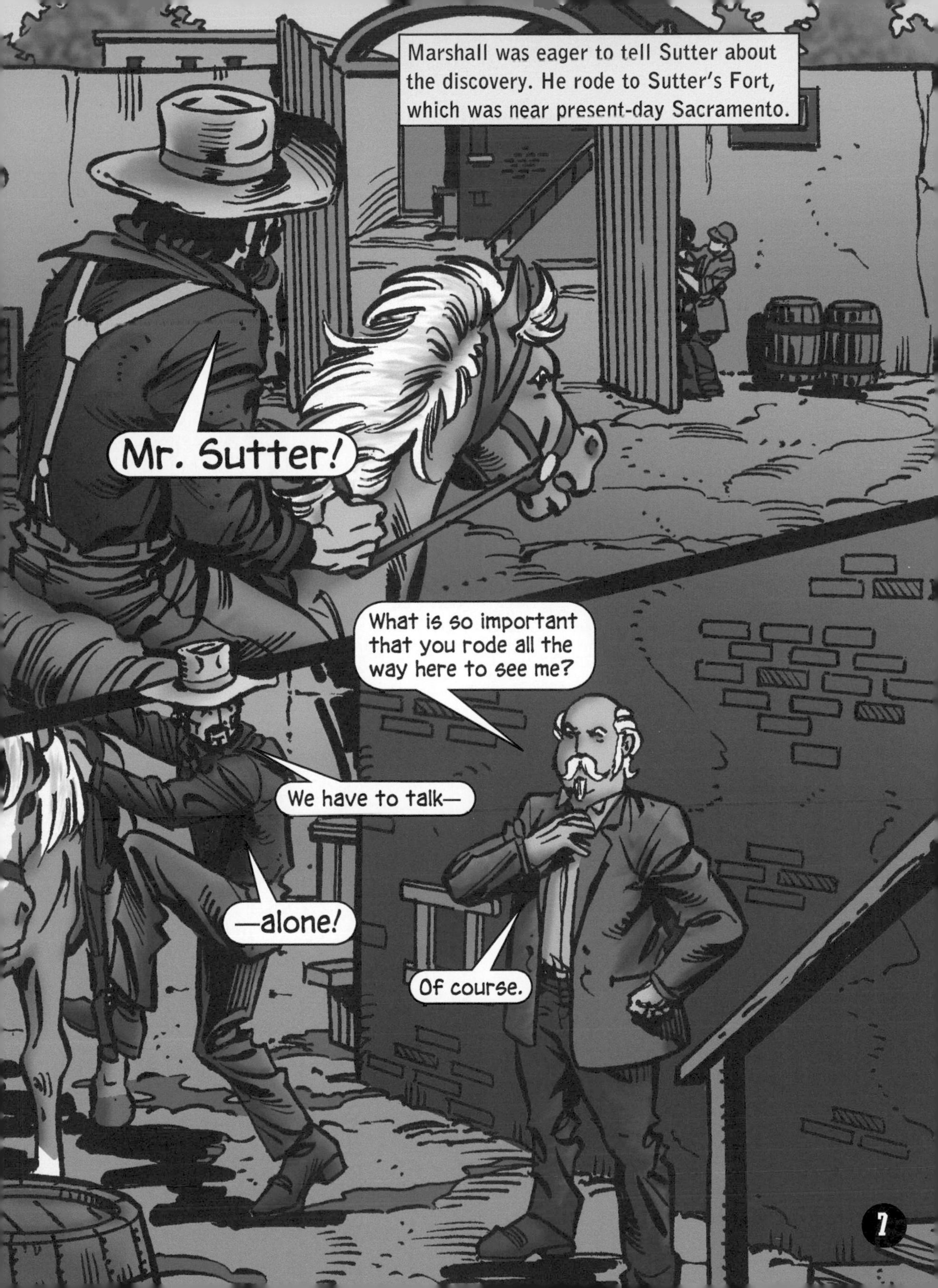
Marshall was eager to tell Sutter about the discovery. He rode to Sutter's Fort, which was near present-day Sacramento.
Mr. Sutter!
What is so important that you rode all the way here to see me?
We have to talk—
—alone!
Of course.

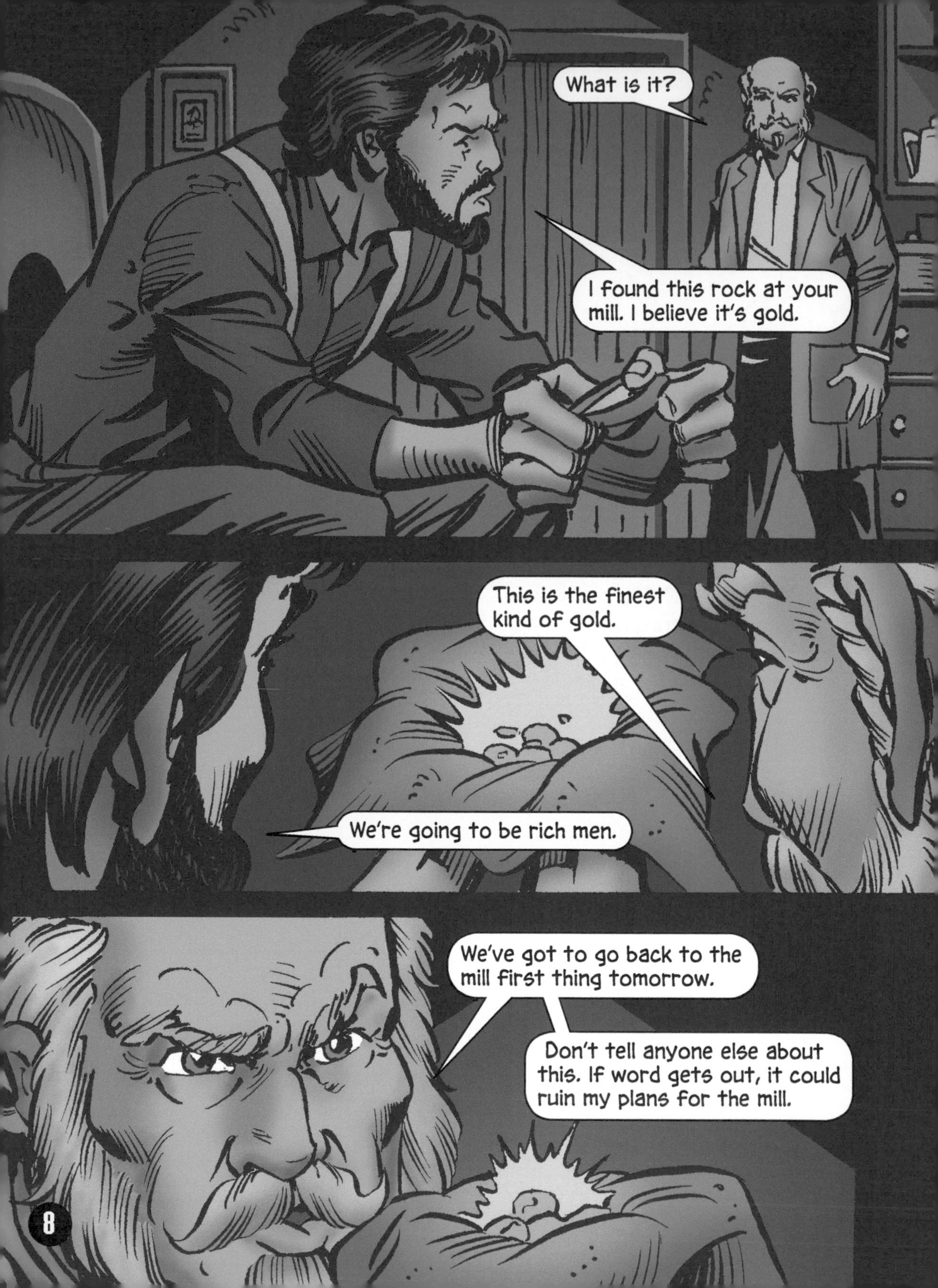
What is it?
I found this rock at your mill. I believe it's gold.
This is the finest kind of gold.
We're going to be rich men.
We've got to go back to the mill first thing tomorrow.
Don't tell anyone else about this. If word gets out, it could ruin my plans for the mill.

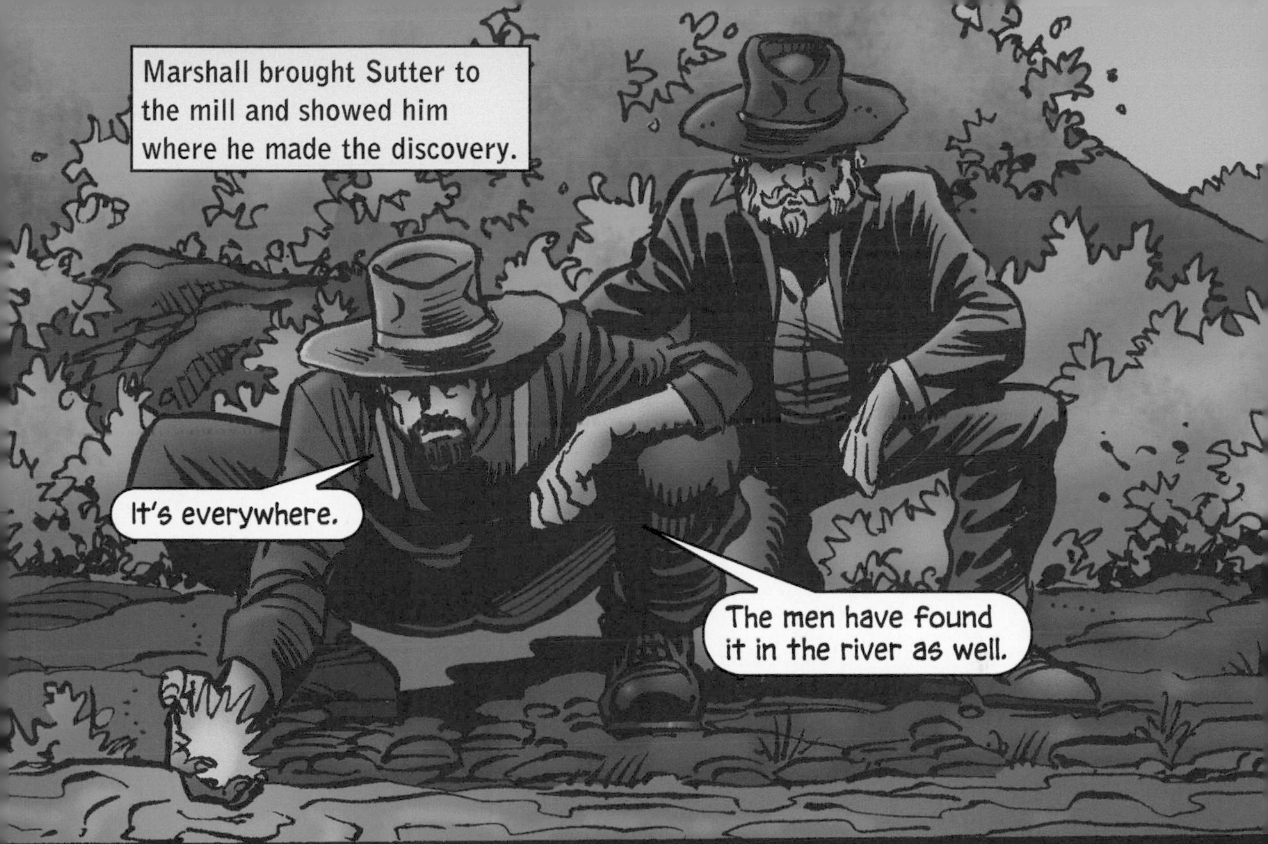
Marshall brought Sutter to the mill and showed him where he made the discovery.
It's everywhere.
The men have found it in the river as well.

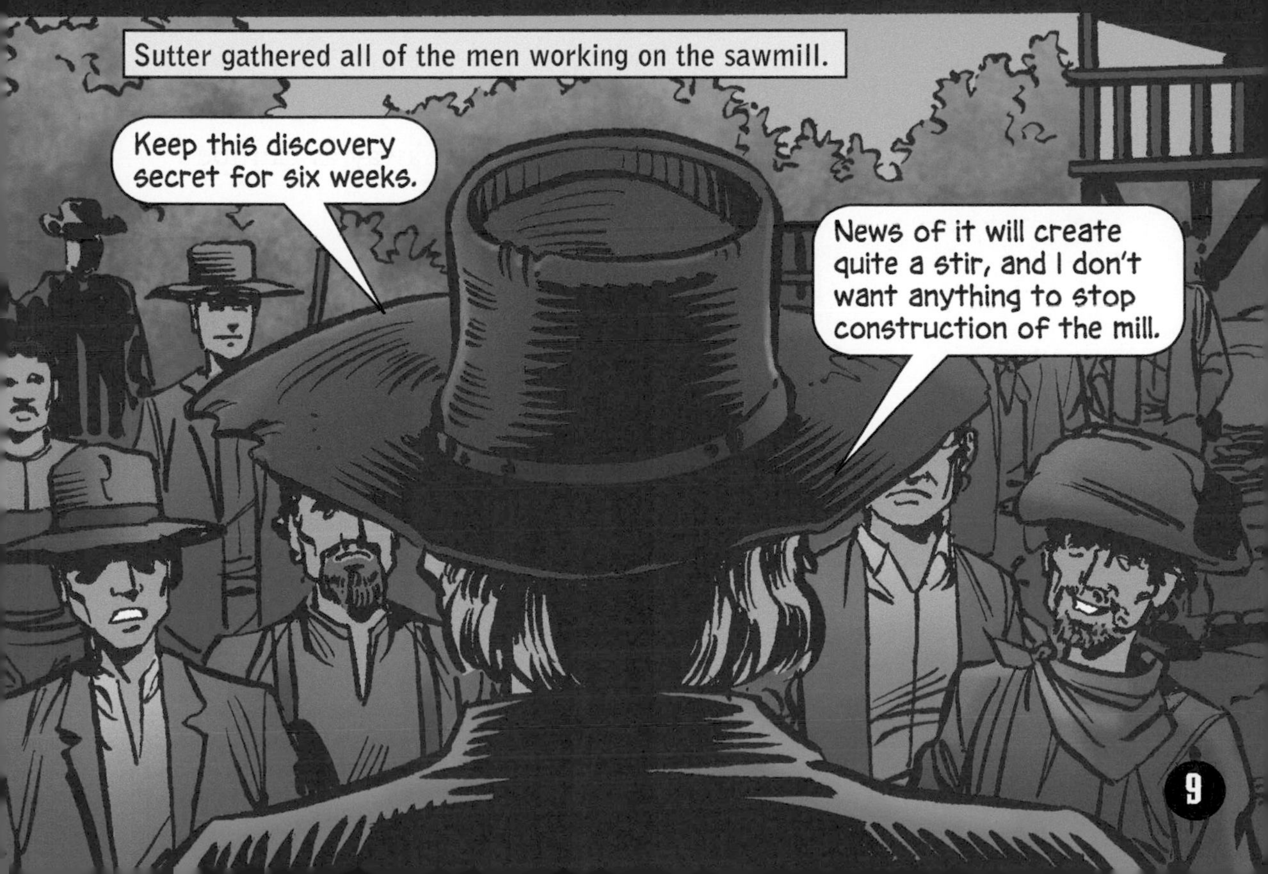
Sutter gathered all of the men working on the sawmill.
Keep this discovery secret for six weeks.
News of it will create quite a stir, and I don't want anything to stop construction of the mill.

Chapter 2: The Secret Is Out

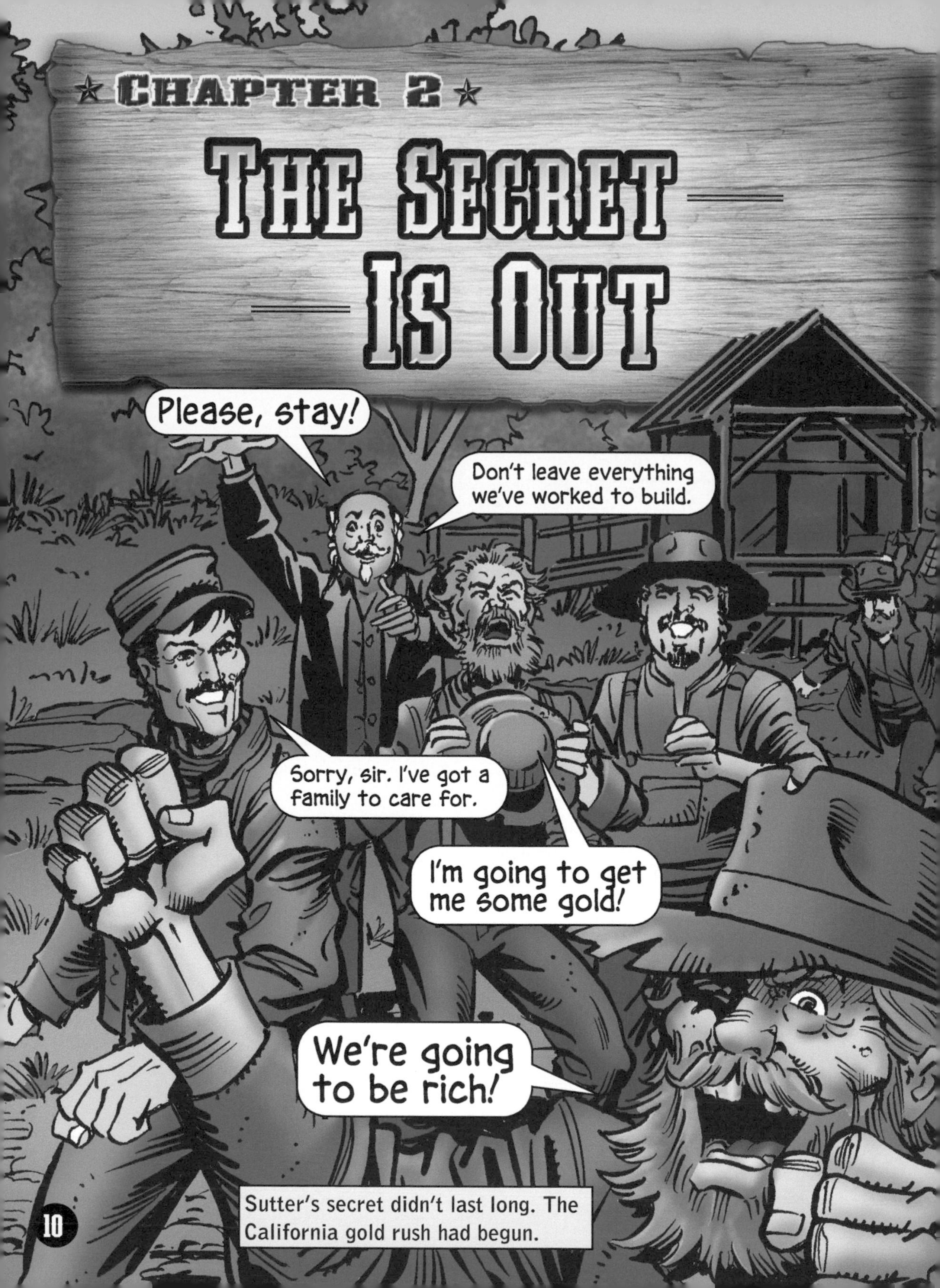
Please, stay!
Don't leave everything we've worked to build.
Sorry, sir. I've got a family to care for.
I'm going to get me some gold!
We're going to be rich!
Sutter's secret didn't last long. The California gold rush had begun.

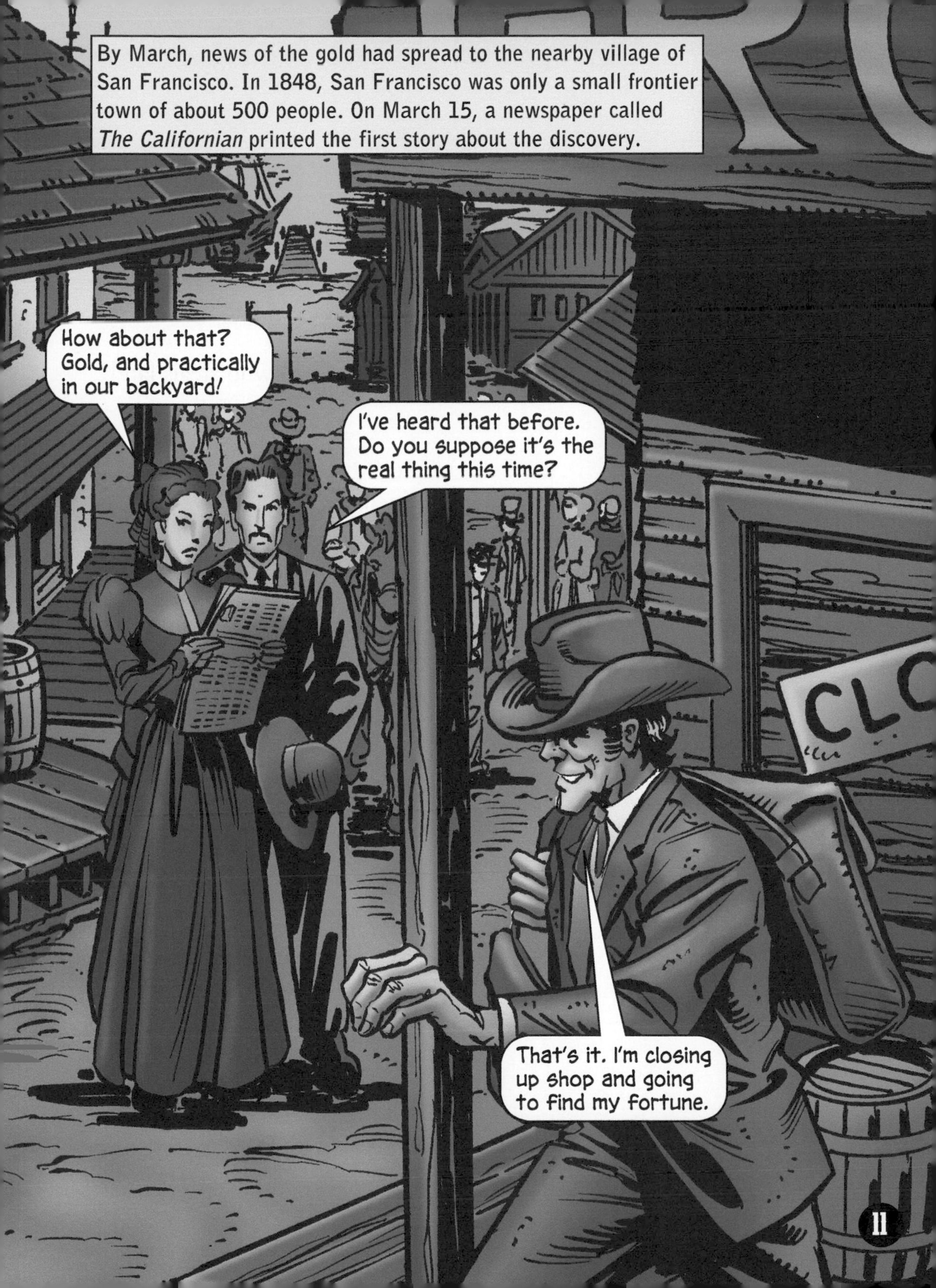
By March, news of the gold had spread to the nearby village of San Francisco. In 1848, San Francisco was only a small frontier town of about 500 people. On March 15, a newspaper called *The Californian* printed the first story about the discovery.
How about that? Gold, and practically in our backyard!
I've heard that before. Do you suppose it's the real thing this time?
That's it. I'm closing up shop and going to find my fortune.

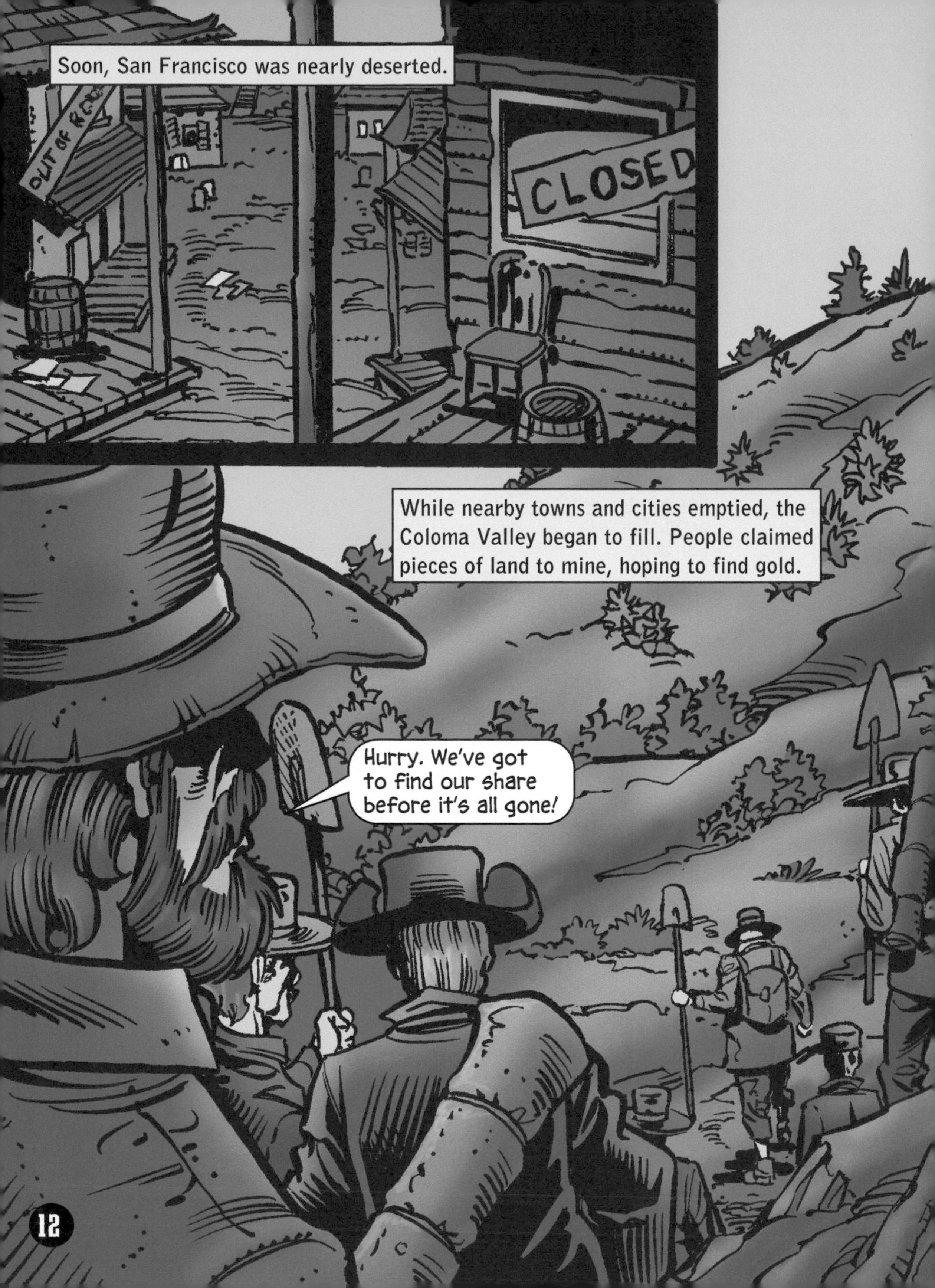

Soon, San Francisco was nearly deserted.
CLOSED
While nearby towns and cities emptied, the Coloma Valley began to fill. People claimed pieces of land to mine, hoping to find gold.
Hurry. We've got to find our share before it's all gone!

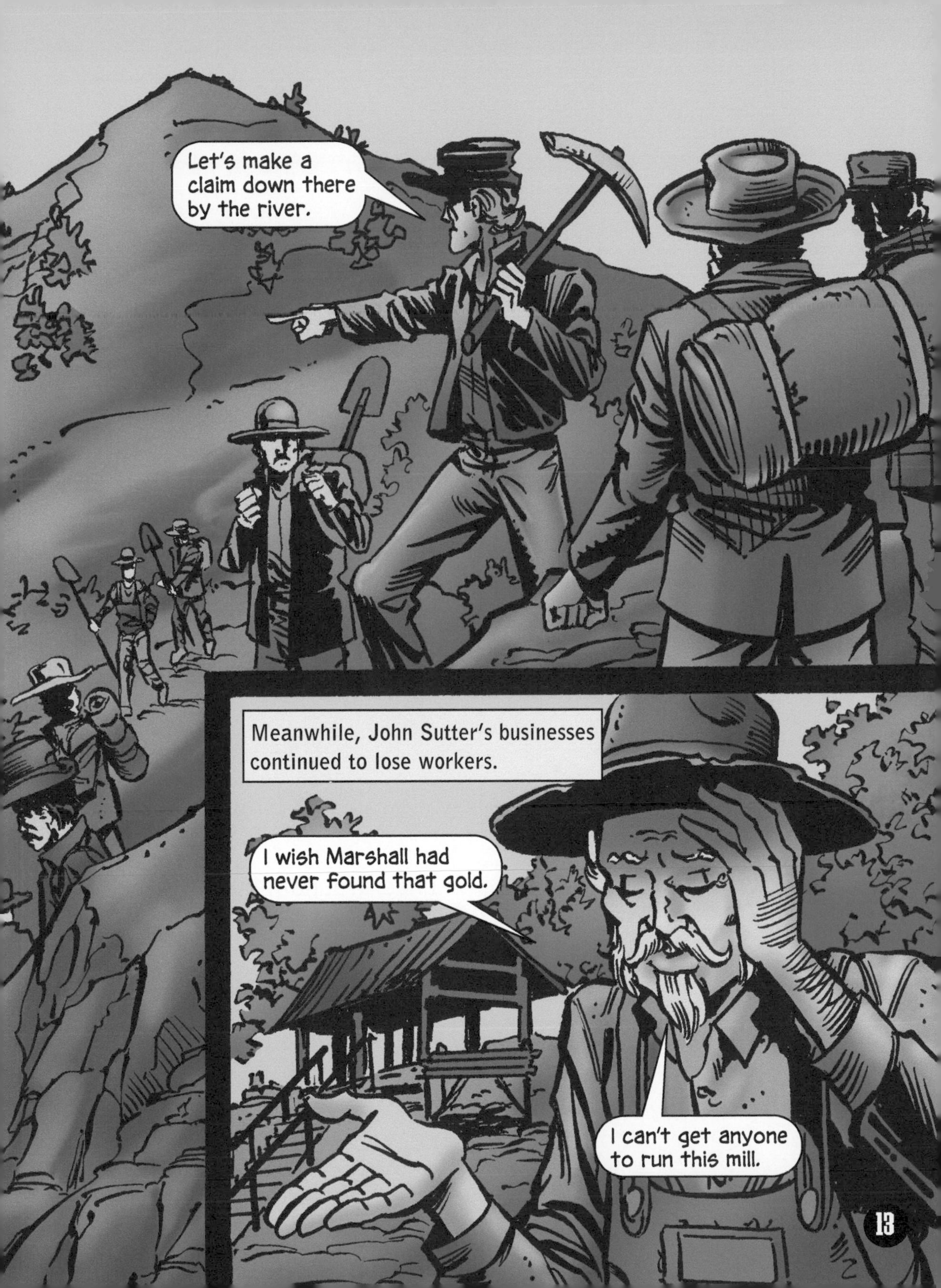
Let's make a claim down there by the river.
Meanwhile, John Sutter's businesses continued to lose workers.
I wish Marshall had never found that gold.
I can't get anyone to run this mill.

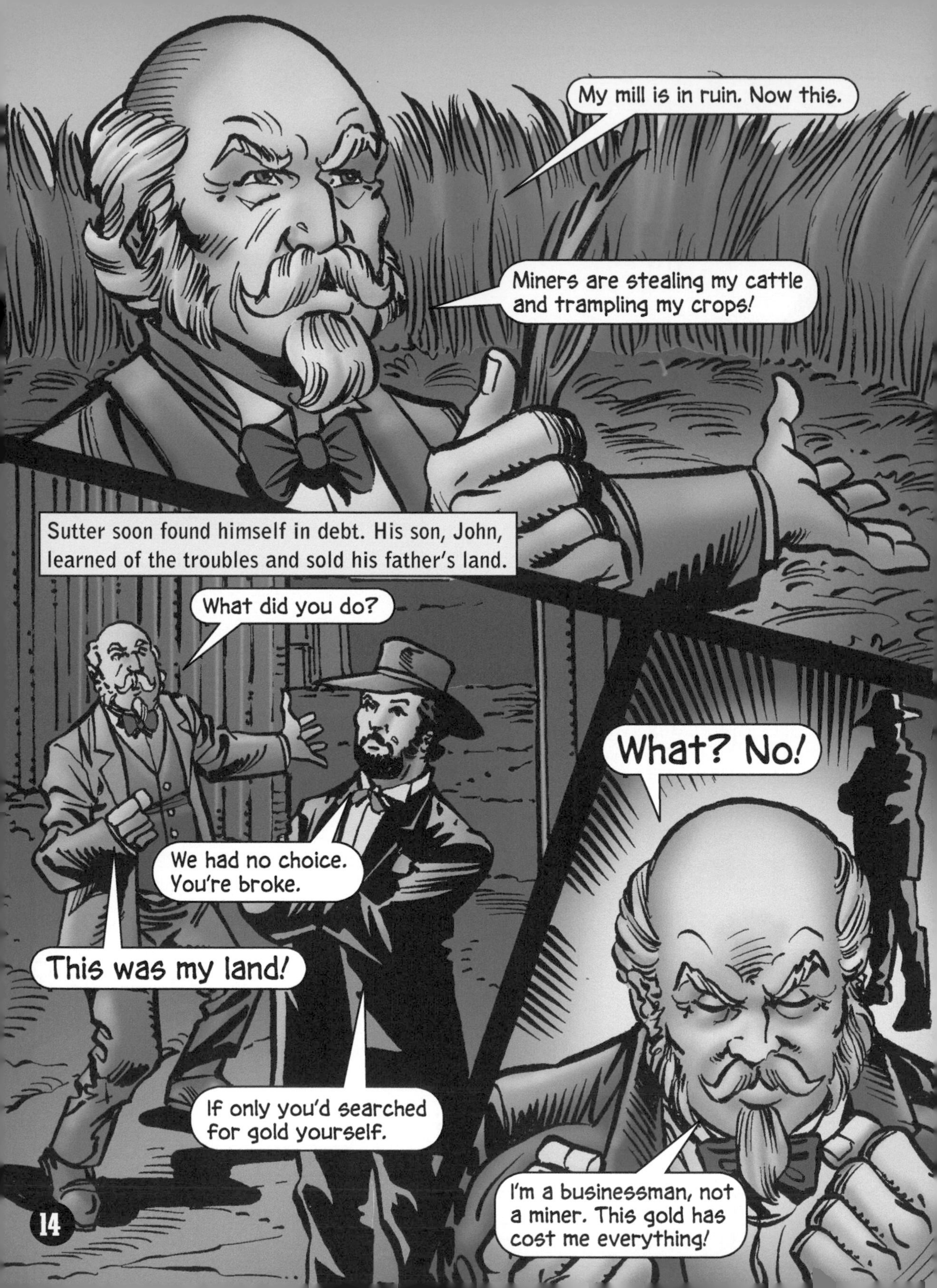
My mill is in ruin. Now this.
Miners are stealing my cattle and trampling my crops!
Sutter soon found himself in debt. His son, John, learned of the troubles and sold his father's land.
What did you do?
We had no choice. You're broke.
This was my land!
If only you'd searched for gold yourself.
What? No!
I'm a businessman, not a miner. This gold has cost me everything!

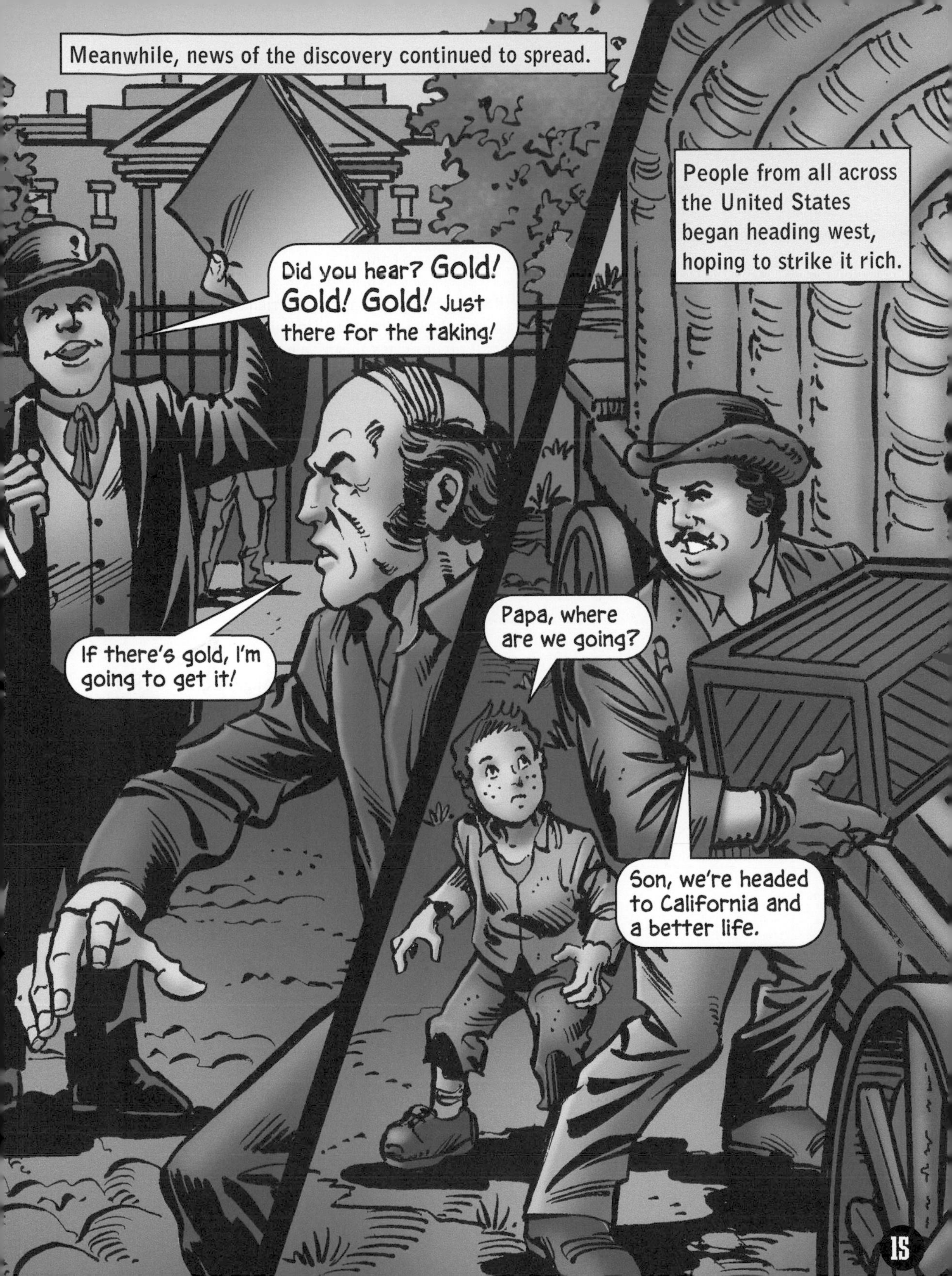
Meanwhile, news of the discovery continued to spread.
Did you hear? Gold! Gold! Gold! Just there for the taking!
If there's gold, I'm going to get it!
People from all across the United States began heading west, hoping to strike it rich.
Papa, where are we going?
Son, we're headed to California and a better life.

Chapter 3

The 49ers

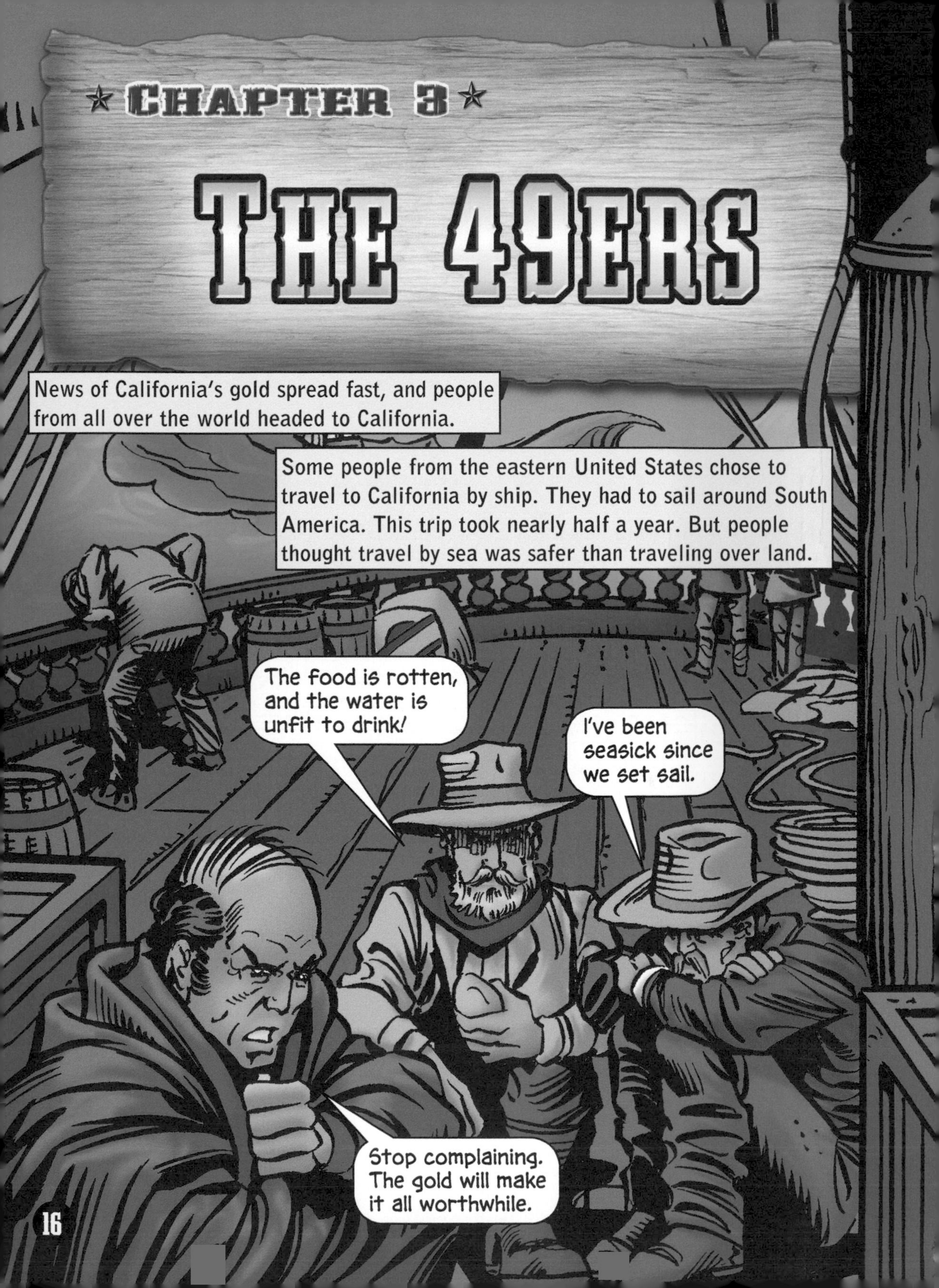
News of California's gold spread fast, and people from all over the world headed to California.
Some people from the eastern United States chose to travel to California by ship. They had to sail around South America. This trip took nearly half a year. But people thought travel by sea was safer than traveling over land.
The food is rotten, and the water is unfit to drink!
I've been seasick since we set sail.
Stop complaining. The gold will make it all worthwhile.

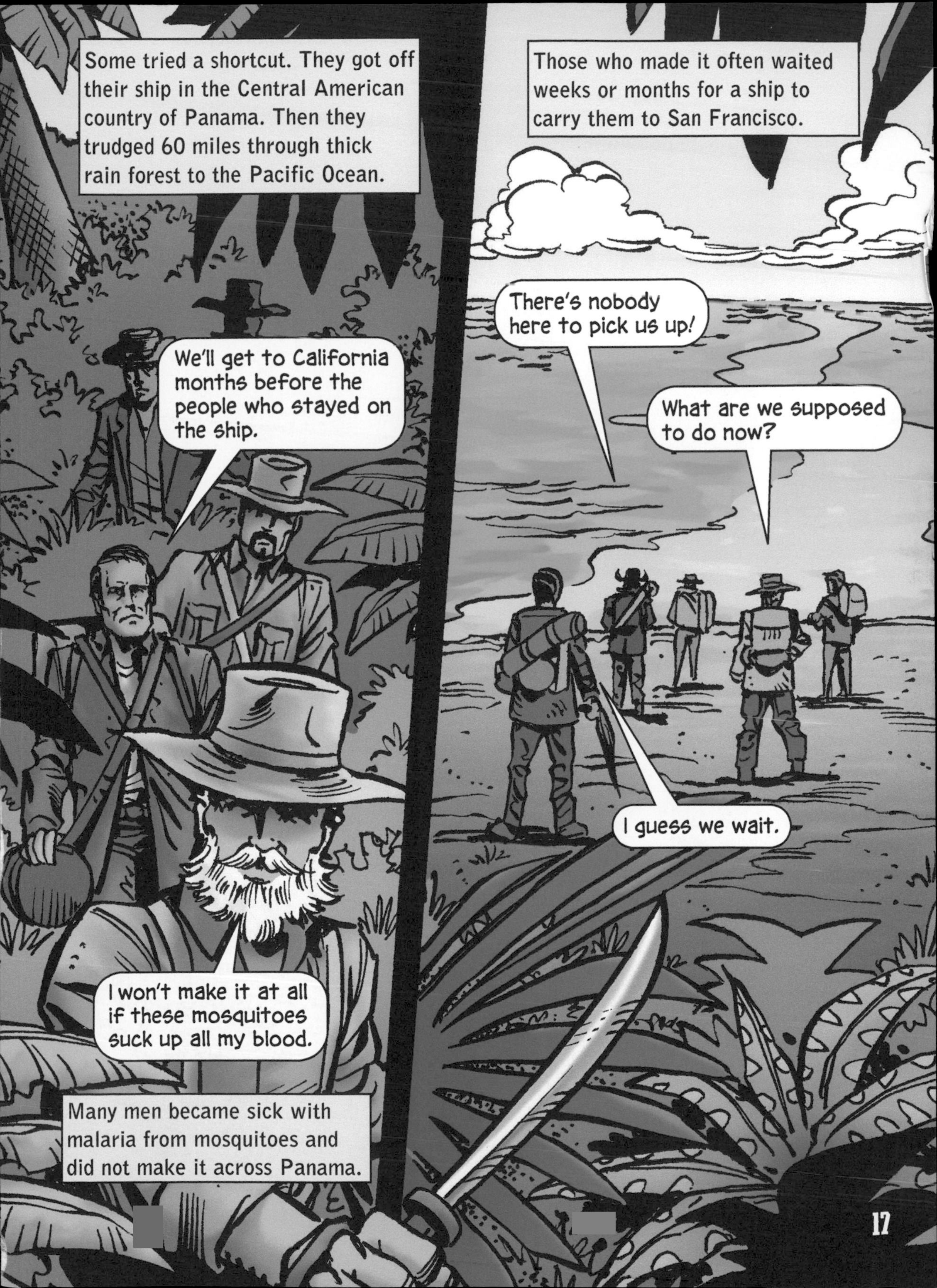

Some tried a shortcut. They got off their ship in the Central American country of Panama. Then they trudged 60 miles through thick rain forest to the Pacific Ocean.
We'll get to California months before the people who stayed on the ship.
I won't make it at all if these mosquitoes suck up all my blood.
Many men became sick with malaria from mosquitoes and did not make it across Panama.
Those who made it often waited weeks or months for a ship to carry them to San Francisco.
There's nobody here to pick us up!
What are we supposed to do now?
I guess we wait.

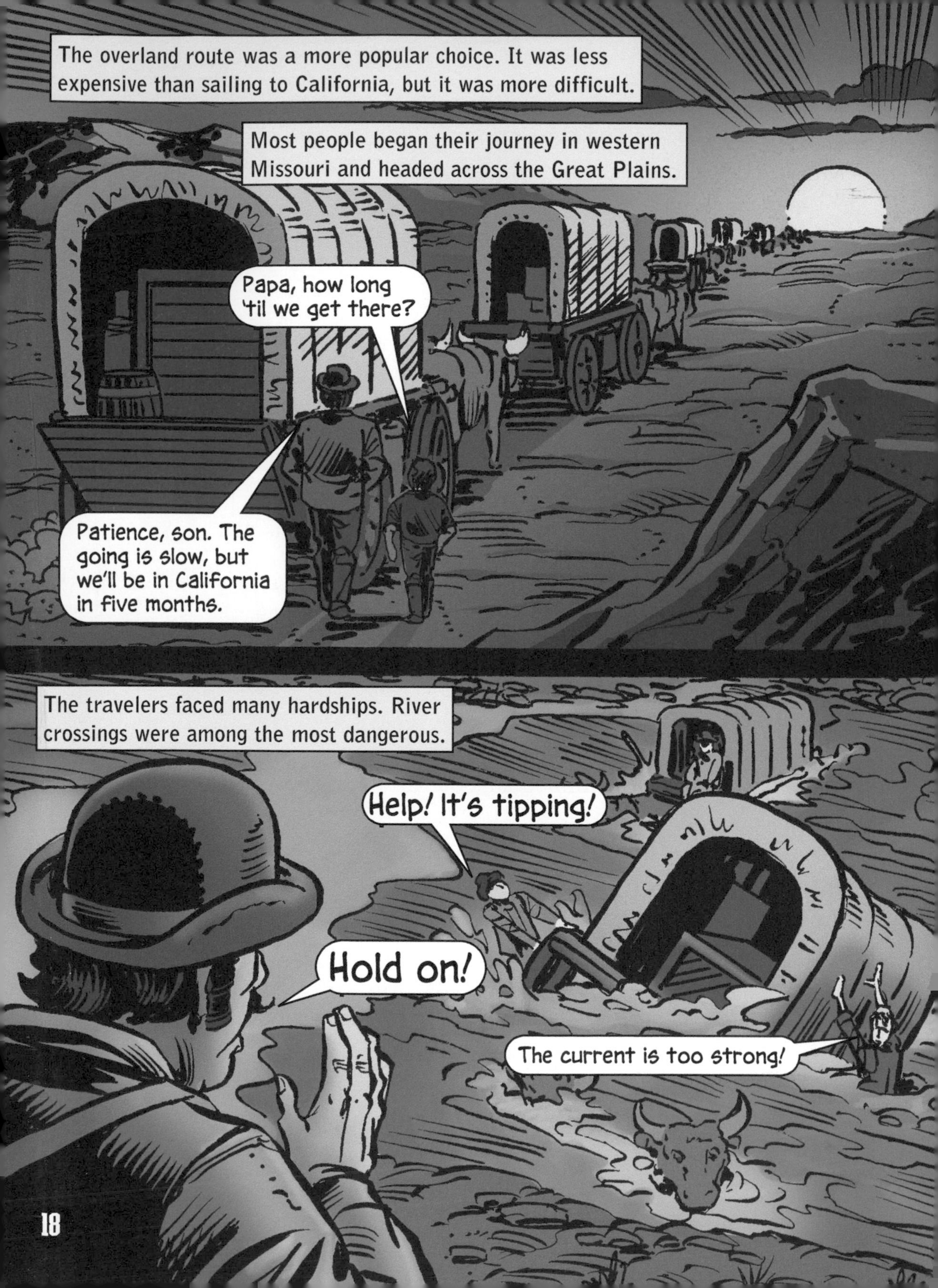
The overland route was a more popular choice. It was less expensive than sailing to California, but it was more difficult.
Most people began their journey in western Missouri and headed across the Great Plains.
Papa, how long 'til we get there?
Patience, son. The going is slow, but we'll be in California in five months.
The travelers faced many hardships. River crossings were among the most dangerous.
Help! It's tipping!
Hold on!
The current is too strong!

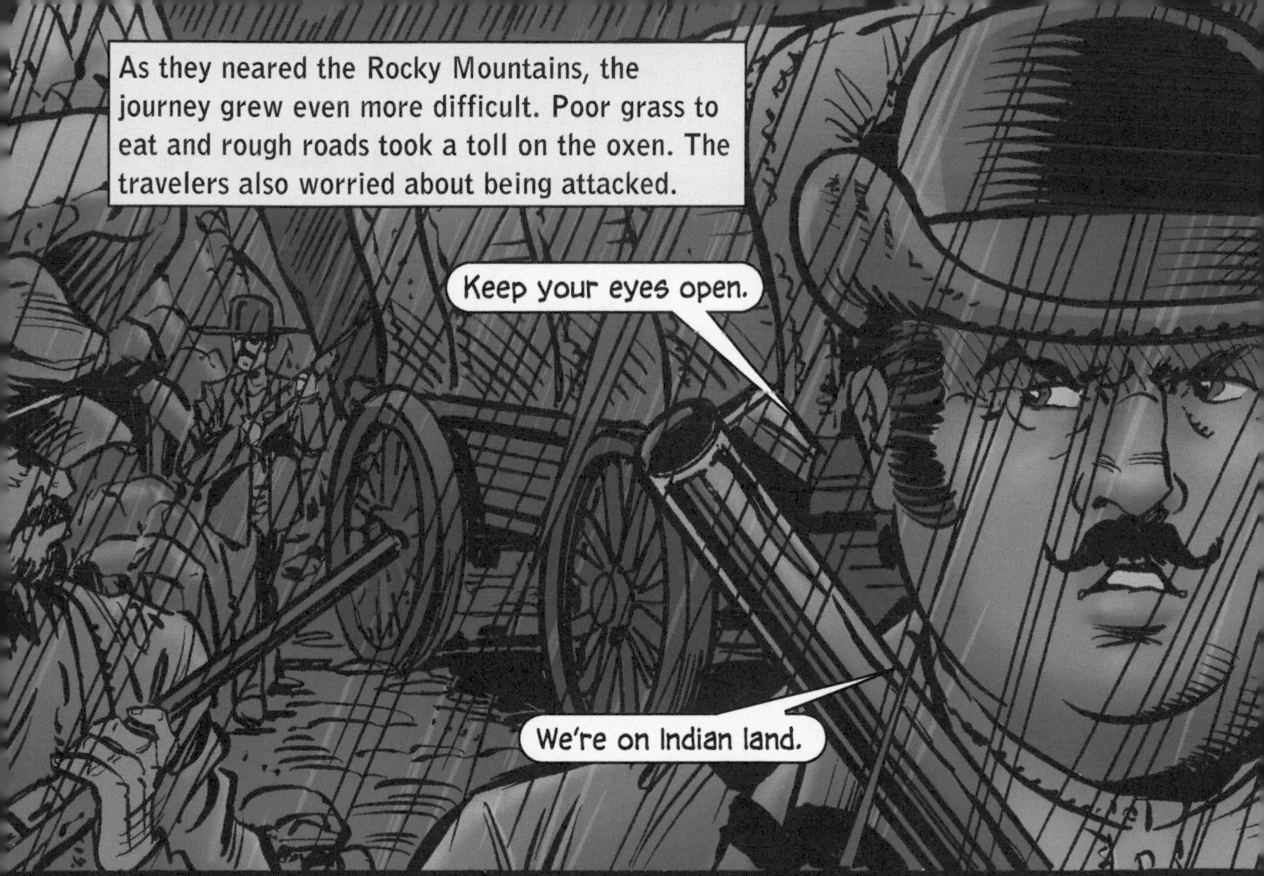
As they neared the Rocky Mountains, the journey grew even more difficult. Poor grass to eat and rough roads took a toll on the oxen. The travelers also worried about being attacked.
Keep your eyes open.
We're on Indian land.

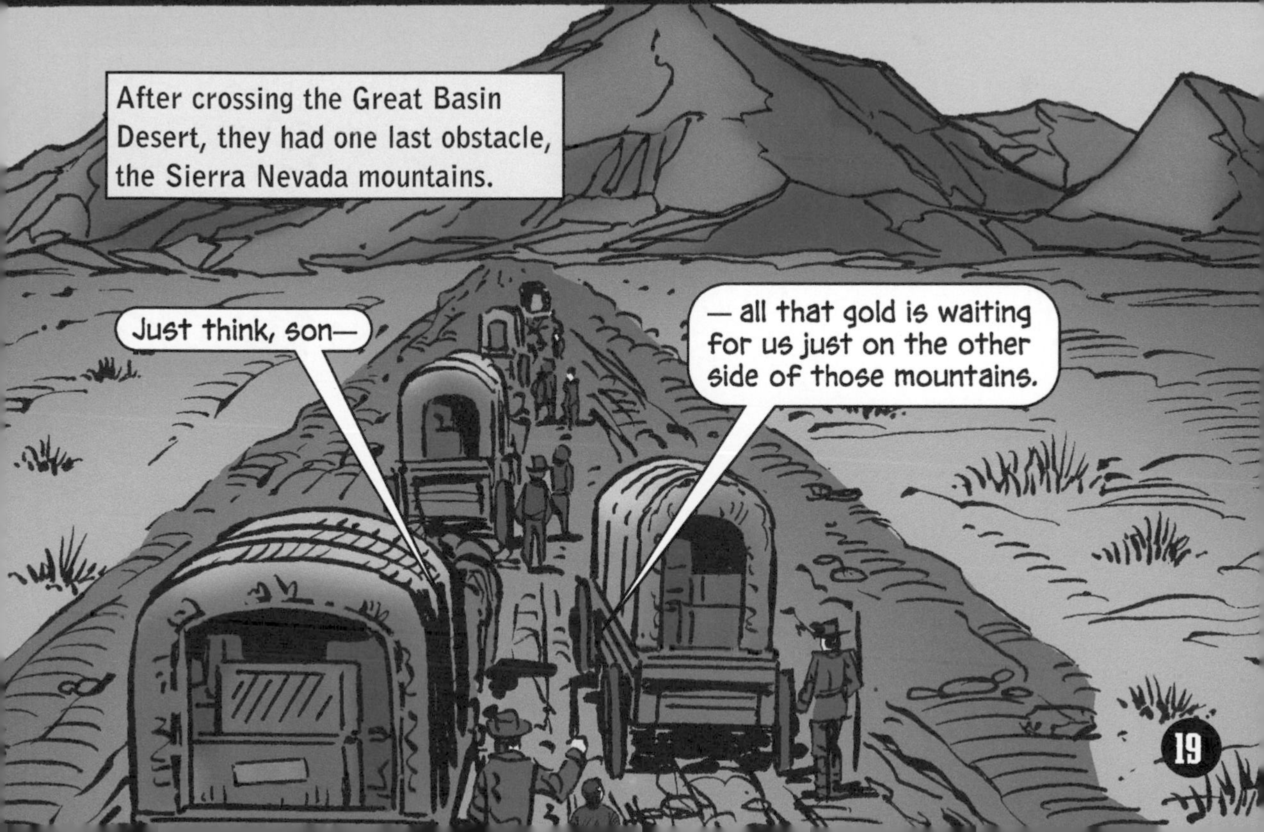
After crossing the Great Basin Desert, they had one last obstacle, the Sierra Nevada mountains.
Just think, son—
— all that gold is waiting for us just on the other side of those mountains.

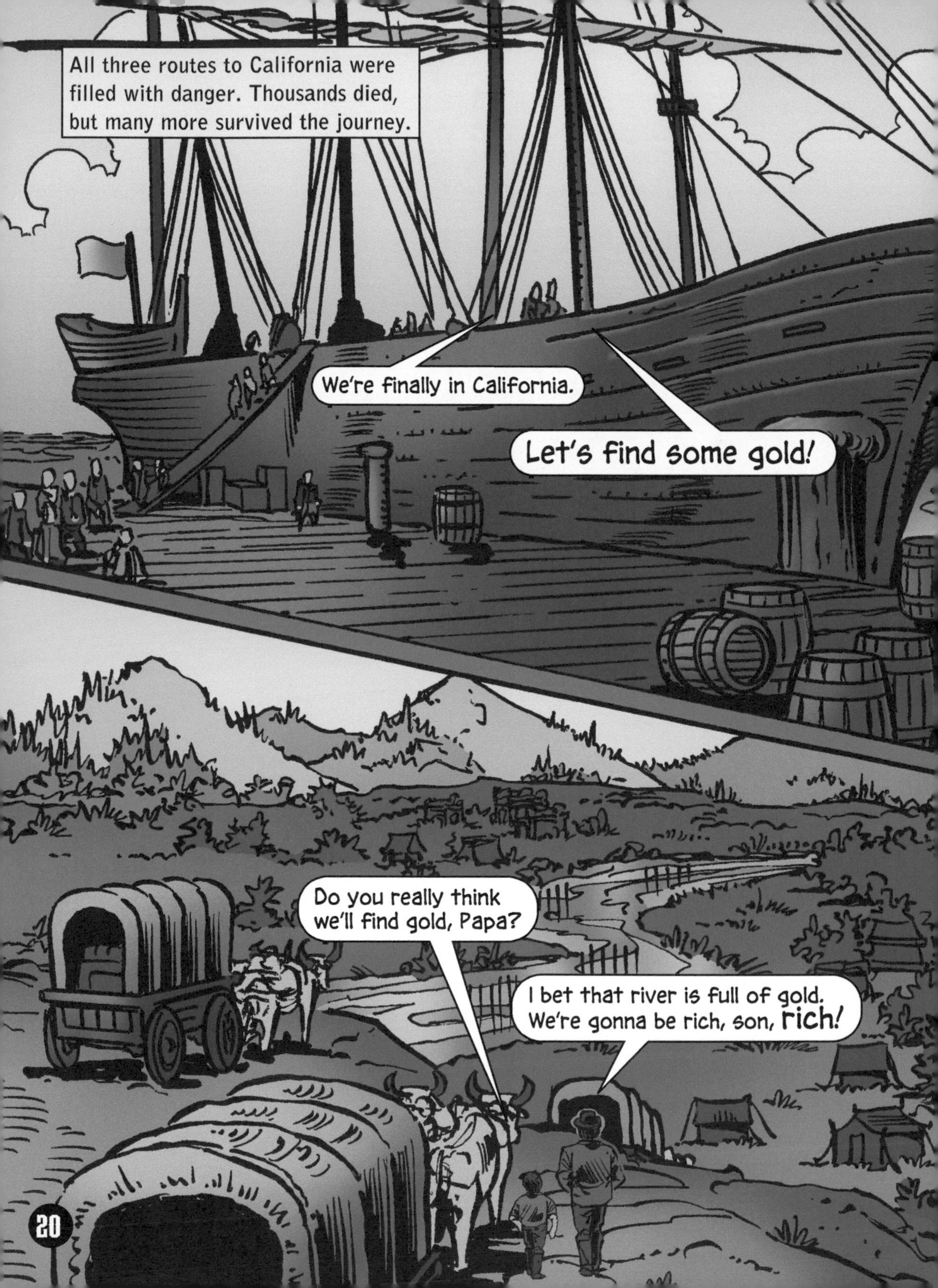
All three routes to California were filled with danger. Thousands died, but many more survived the journey.
We're finally in California.
Let's find some gold!
Do you really think we'll find gold, Papa?
I bet that river is full of gold. We're gonna be rich, son, rich!

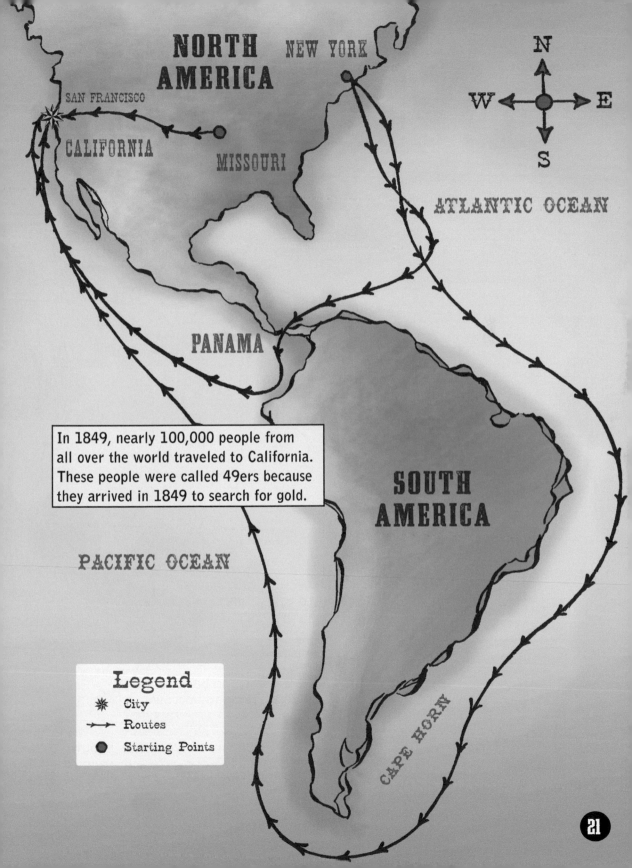

NORTH AMERICA

NEW YORK

SAN FRANCISCO

CALIFORNIA

MISSOURI

PANAMA

ATLANTIC OCEAN

SOUTH AMERICA

PACIFIC OCEAN

CAPE HORN

In 1849, nearly 100,000 people from all over the world traveled to California. These people were called 49ers because they arrived in 1849 to search for gold.

Legend
✳ City
→ Routes
● Starting Points

Chapter 4
The Search for Gold

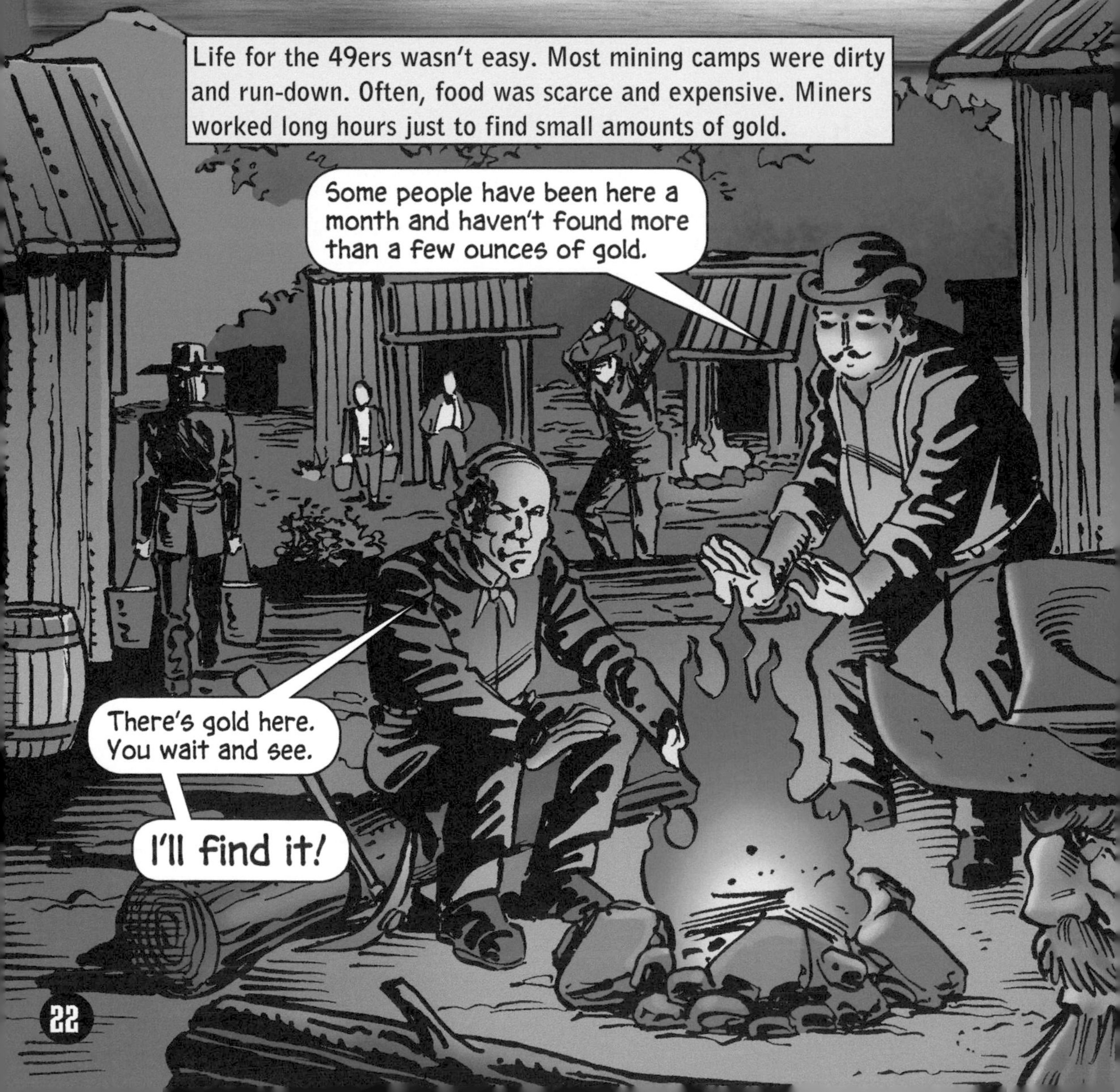
Life for the 49ers wasn't easy. Most mining camps were dirty and run-down. Often, food was scarce and expensive. Miners worked long hours just to find small amounts of gold.
Some people have been here a month and haven't found more than a few ounces of gold.
There's gold here. You wait and see.
I'll find it!

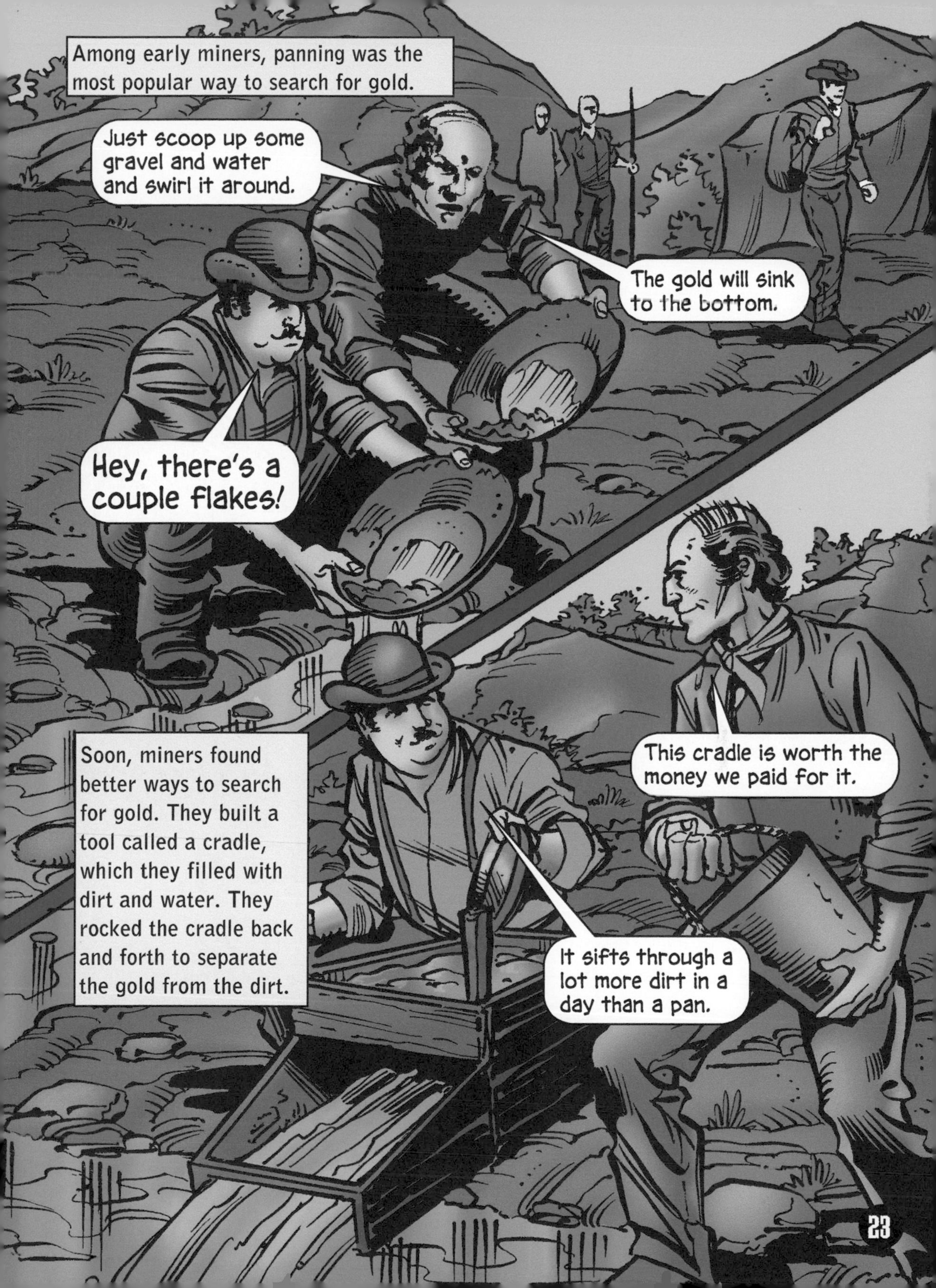
Among early miners, panning was the most popular way to search for gold.
Just scoop up some gravel and water and swirl it around.
The gold will sink to the bottom.
Hey, there's a couple flakes!
Soon, miners found better ways to search for gold. They built a tool called a cradle, which they filled with dirt and water. They rocked the cradle back and forth to separate the gold from the dirt.
This cradle is worth the money we paid for it.
It sifts through a lot more dirt in a day than a pan.

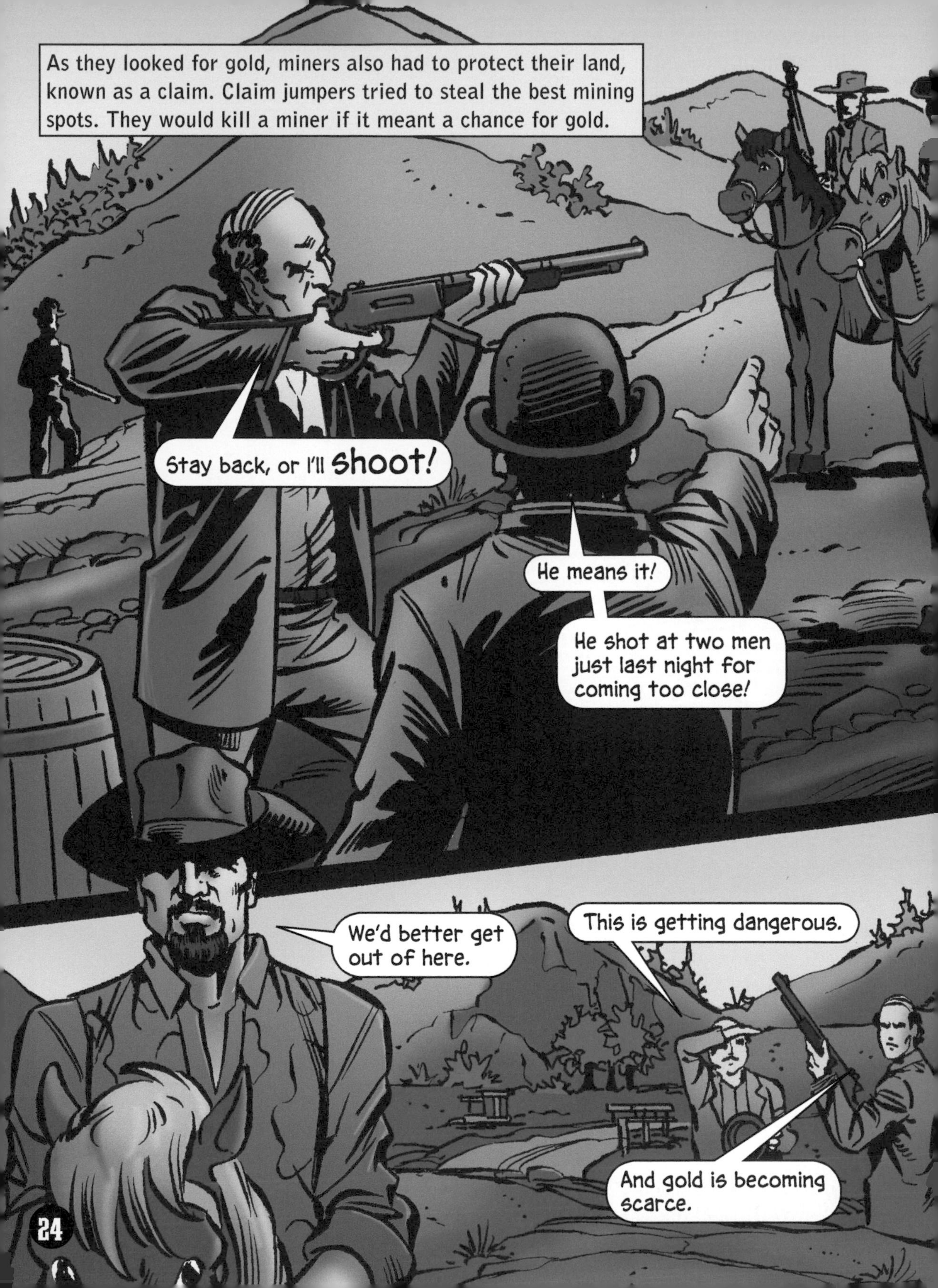
As they looked for gold, miners also had to protect their land, known as a claim. Claim jumpers tried to steal the best mining spots. They would kill a miner if it meant a chance for gold.
Stay back, or I'll SHOOT!
He means it!
He shot at two men just last night for coming too close!
We'd better get out of here.
This is getting dangerous.
And gold is becoming scarce.

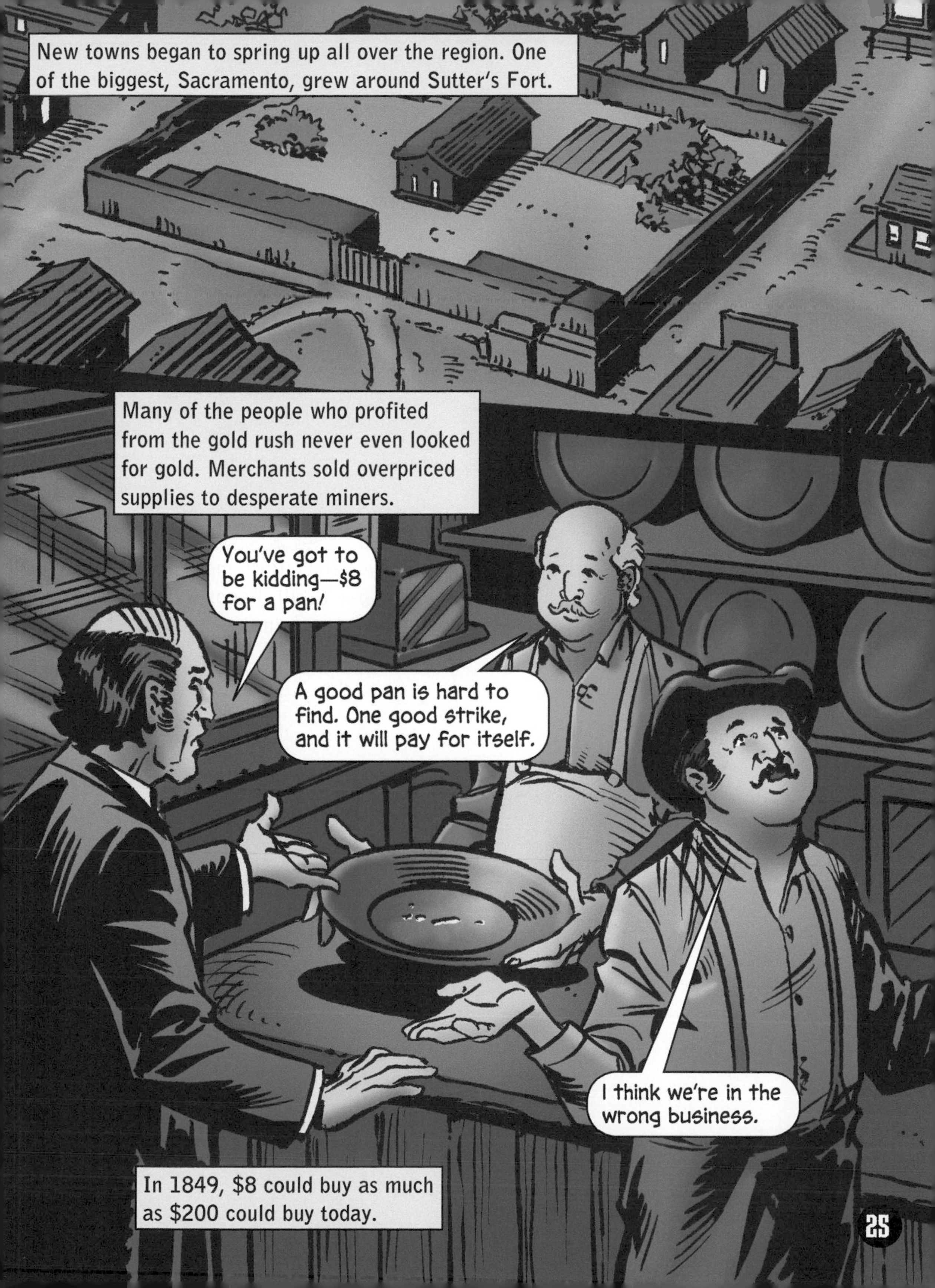
New towns began to spring up all over the region. One of the biggest, Sacramento, grew around Sutter's Fort.
Many of the people who profited from the gold rush never even looked for gold. Merchants sold overpriced supplies to desperate miners.
You've got to be kidding—$8 for a pan!
A good pan is hard to find. One good strike, and it will pay for itself.
I think we're in the wrong business.
In 1849, $8 could buy as much as $200 could buy today.

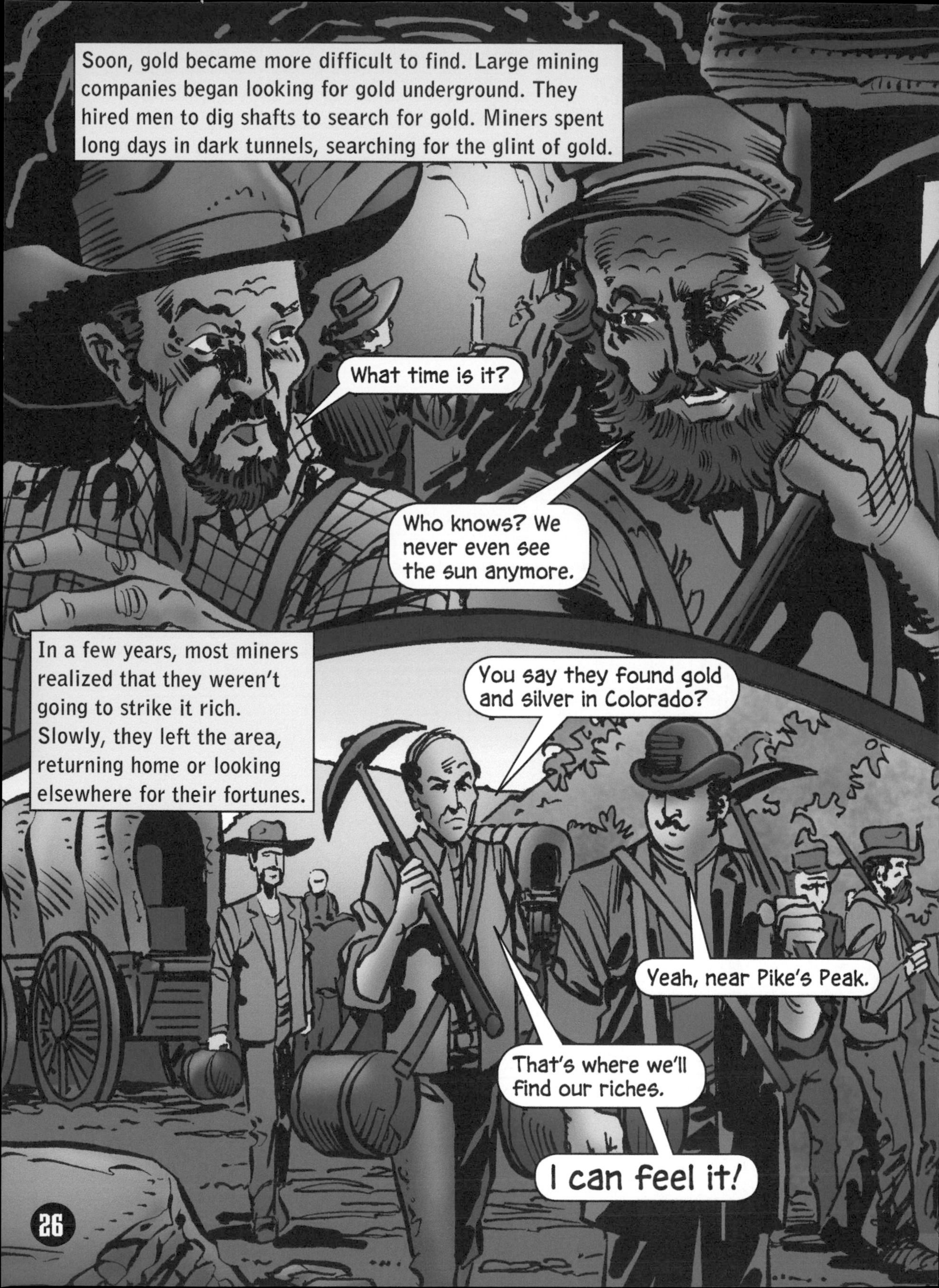
Soon, gold became more difficult to find. Large mining companies began looking for gold underground. They hired men to dig shafts to search for gold. Miners spent long days in dark tunnels, searching for the glint of gold.
What time is it?
Who knows? We never even see the sun anymore.
In a few years, most miners realized that they weren't going to strike it rich. Slowly, they left the area, returning home or looking elsewhere for their fortunes.
You say they found gold and silver in Colorado?
Yeah, near Pike's Peak.
That's where we'll find our riches.
I can feel it!

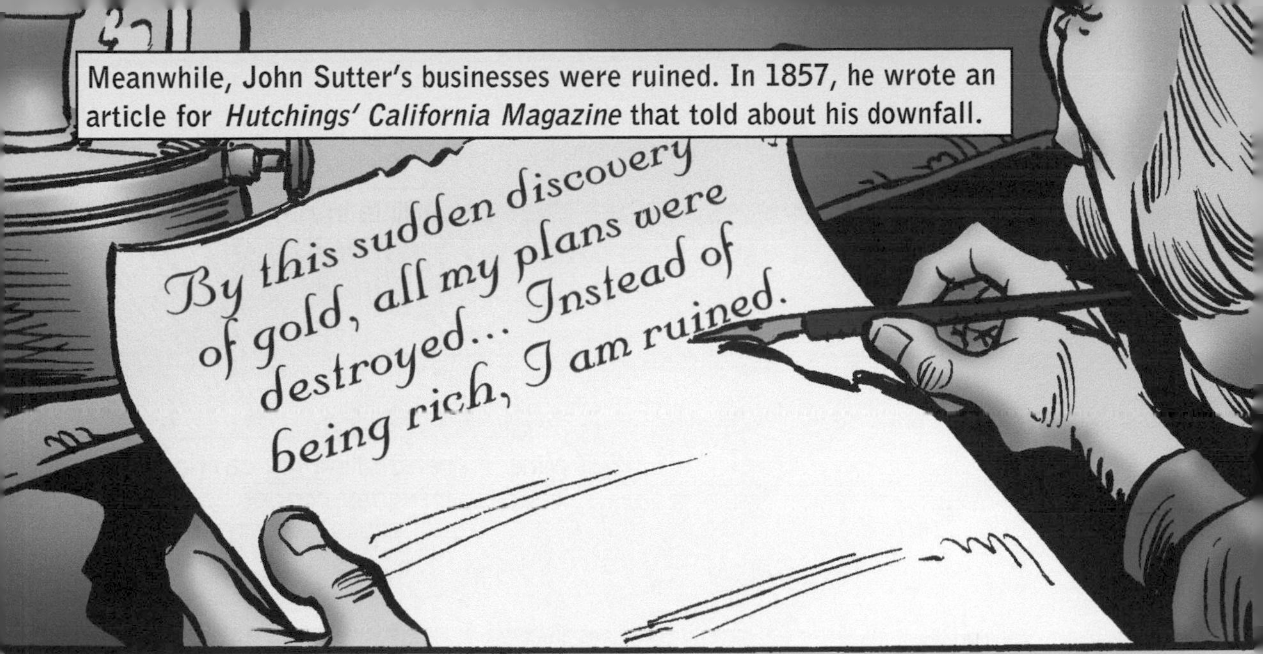
Meanwhile, John Sutter's businesses were ruined. In 1857, he wrote an article for *Hutchings' California Magazine* that told about his downfall.
By this sudden discovery of gold, all my plans were destroyed... Instead of being rich, I am ruined.

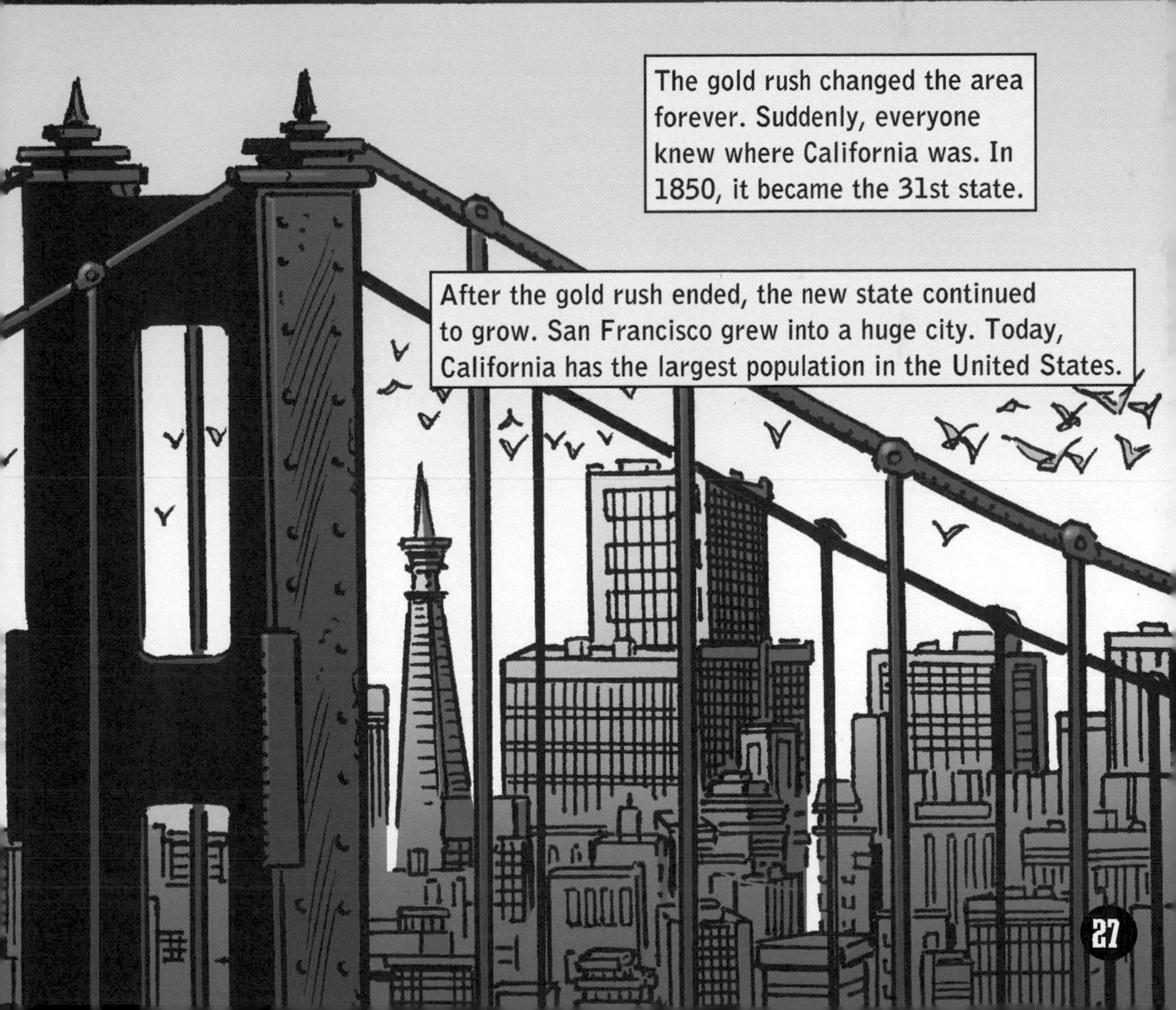
The gold rush changed the area forever. Suddenly, everyone knew where California was. In 1850, it became the 31st state.
After the gold rush ended, the new state continued to grow. San Francisco grew into a huge city. Today, California has the largest population in the United States.

★ MORE ABOUT THE ★ GOLD RUSH

- In January 1848, California was not yet a part of the United States. The United States had just defeated Mexico in the Mexican War (1846–1848). The two countries were working on a peace treaty that would give the territory of California to the United States. At the time, neither government knew about the gold. California was admitted as a state in 1850.

- Miners came to California from all over the world. Many early miners crossed the border from Mexico. People sailed from China to search for gold. Even people as far away as Europe came to California, dreaming of riches.

- About one out of 10 people who took the overland route to California died along the way. Cholera was one of the most common causes of death. Travelers got cholera from drinking polluted water.

- A woman named Margaret Frink made a fortune during the gold rush. But she never looked for gold. She cooked and sold food to hungry miners. She said she sold $18,000 worth of pies. That amount would be almost $400,000 in today's money.

- When the gold rush started, San Francisco had only about 500 people. At first, many people left town to search for their fortunes. But the town wasn't deserted for long. By 1849, so many people arrived in the area that more than 20,000 people lived in San Francisco.

- The discovery of gold was so important to California's development that today it is called the Golden State.

- During the gold rush, two men, Henry Wells and William Fargo, decided to start a bank for miners. Today, Wells Fargo is one of the largest banking companies in the world.

- In 1853, mining companies started using hydraulic mining. This destructive mining method used powerful jets of water to tear up land. The jets were so strong that they could kill a person from 200 feet (61 meters) away. Thirty years later, hydraulic mining was banned.

- Many small towns started as the 49ers rushed into California. After the gold rush was over, some of these towns were abandoned. They became ghost towns. Some ghost towns still stand today.

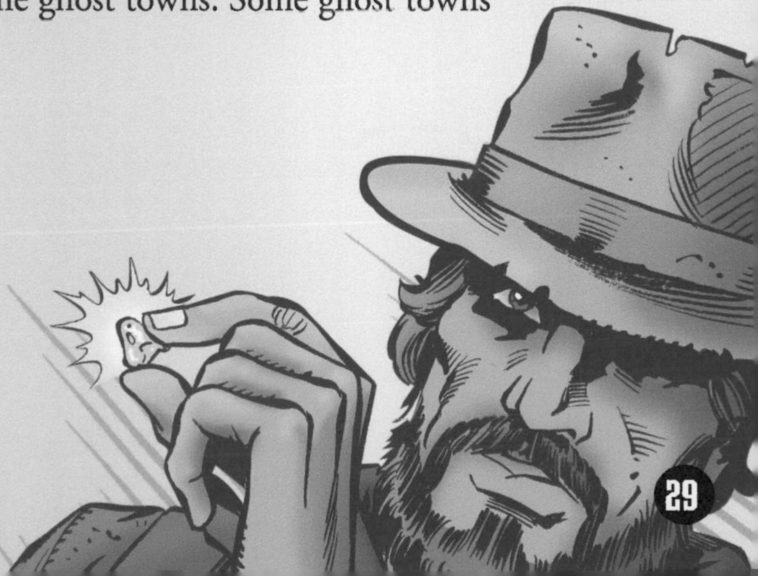

GLOSSARY

cholera (KOL-ur-uh)—a disease that causes severe sickness and diarrhea; the main cause of cholera during the gold rush was polluted water.

claim jumper (KLAYM JUHM-pur)—a person who steals land that belongs to someone else

malaria (muh-LAIR-ee-uh)—a tropical disease people get from mosquito bites; symptoms include chills, fever, and sweating.

millrace (MIL-rayss)—a trench that allows water to travel from a river to a mill

sawmill (SAW-mil)—a place where people use machines to saw logs into boards

INTERNET SITES

FactHound offers a safe, fun way to find Internet sites related to this book. All of the sites on FactHound have been researched by our staff.

Here's how:

1. *Visit www.facthound.com*
2. Type in this special code **0736843701** for age-appropriate sites. Or enter a search word related to this book for a more general search.
3. Click on the **Fetch It** button.

FactHound will fetch the best sites for you!

READ MORE

Blashfield, Jean F. *The California Gold Rush.* We the People. Minneapolis: Compass Point Books, 2001.

Crewe, Sabrina, and Michael V. Uschan. *The California Gold Rush.* Events That Shaped America. Milwaukee: Gareth Stevens, 2003.

Gregory, Kristiana. *Seeds of Hope: The Gold Rush Diary of Susanna Fairchild, California Territory, 1849.* Dear America. New York: Scholastic, 2001.

Hayhurst, Chris. *John Sutter: California Pioneer.* Primary Sources of Famous People in American History. New York: Rosen, 2004.

BIBLIOGRAPHY

All about the Gold Rush
http://www.isu.edu/~trinmich/allabout.html.

Boessenecker, John. *Gold Dust and Gunsmoke: Tales of Gold Rush Outlaws, Gunfighters, Lawmen, and Vigilantes.* New York: John Wiley, 1999.

Brands, H. W. *The Age of Gold: The California Gold Rush and the New American Dream.* New York: Doubleday, 2002.

Rau, Margaret. *The Wells Fargo Book of the Gold Rush.* New York: Atheneum, 2001.

INDEX